PRAISE FOR

THE BIZZICS WAY

"Chip Higgins has a heart for business owners, and his coaching, consulting, and mentoring over the years have proven invaluable to his many clients. Now, with this highly readable and engaging book, he offers the insights from forty years of banking experience to anyone who will read and apply the Bizzics tools to their business. I look forward to applying this knowledge to my own business and recommending it to my students and clients."

Dr. Nina J. Morel, EdD, PCC

Professor; Executive Director of Coaching and Leadership Development

"Chip Higgins understands how small businesses work ... and don't. As a banker, he's lent them money. As business owner, he's counseled them. As an author, he has merged practices of thriving businesses and immutable laws of physics into memorable, actionable guidance for small business owners who want to launch or expand their businesses."

Nick Miller

President, Clarity Advantage

"Passion is critical to success and mastery. I have personally watched Chip Higgins's passion for serving small business owners grow over the past thirty-seven years. The Bizzics Way is the culmination of that journey. In it, Chip lays out the critical business principles required for any business owner to maximize momentum and, perhaps more importantly, provides the practical insights needed to implement them in your business."

Terry Turner

Founder and CEO, Pinnacle Financial Partners

"Chip Higgins sets the scene wherever he goes. His spirit to help others and his experience in business almost immediately builds trust. What better person to write a book about stepping outside the box of 'business?' Chip's focus is on people, their energy, and building culture and trust—whether a teammate or a customer. A force of nature in the gentlest of ways, Chip always puts people first. For 15 years Chip has been available to me to advise, mentor, and support my small business. I'm so excited for him to share his knowledge and energy to help others grow their business, as he has helped me grow mine."

Heather Gee-Thomas

Founding Partner, G Squared Wireless

"Right from the onset, Chip tells us that he became a banker because he saw the important role bankers played in his community. He says, 'It was the way the bankers I knew contributed to the neighborhood and built it up.' Forty-plus years later, Chip is still passionate about the way business leaders are contributing and building neighborhoods. The Bizzics Way is a love letter from a tireless and passionate advocate for leaders. Here is wisdom from someone who believes that small business leaders deserve the wisdom big business can access with their big budgets. In this book, you will glean applicable wisdom from someone who appreciates the struggles and promises of the small business, nonprofit, or budding leader. My colleagues and I work in the nonprofit sector in rural Uganda and are beneficiaries of these practical ideas. Chip draws on universal laws of physics such as energy, velocity, momentum, and so forth to drive home principles that deliver success regardless of the size of organization, mission, or geographical region. Chip provides a great deal of insight into why small business entrepreneurs exist, debunks the myths, and removes the excuses around success in business."

David Ssebulime, MDIV

Founding Director, Raise the Roof Academy

"The knowledge I have gained from Chip Higgins has helped me build the confidence and competitive edge I needed to build on my success as a small business owner. In The Bizzics Way, *Chip provides realistic tools for businesses on how to overcome common small business challenges. Chip says it all here: 'The right resources and coaching can be game-changing for small business owners.'* The Bizzics Way, *it provides real life examples and exercises to challenge the reader and provide solutions."*

Katie Conner

Owner, iBeach31

"Good leaders provide direction, purpose, and reason for a group or organization to follow. They also share their knowledge, wisdom, and experience with others. After spending many months working directly with Chip Higgins for our businesses funding needs, I can honestly say his understanding of the process from start to finish is what made all the difference. The Bizzics Way *is an entrepreneur's guide to turning a vision into reality!"*

Josh Diamond

Founder and CEO, Diamond Sound Studios

THE BIZZICS WAY

CHIP HIGGINS

THE BIZZICS WAY

POWERING

YOUR

SMALL BUSINESS

TO MAXIMUM

MOMENTUM

Forbes | Books

Published by Forbes Books, Charleston, South Carolina.
An imprint of Advantage Media Group.

Forbes Books is a registered trademark, and the Forbes Books colophon is a trademark of Forbes Media, LLC.

Printed in the United States of America.

10   9   8   7   6   5   4   3   2   1

ISBN: 979-8-88750-328-8 (Hardcover)
ISBN: 979-8-88750-329-5 (eBook)

Library of Congress Control Number: 2023921467

Cover design by David Taylor.
Illustrations by Matthew Morse.
Layout design by Analisa Smith.

This custom publication is intended to provide accurate information and the opinions of the author in regard to the subject matter covered. It is sold with the understanding that the publisher, Forbes Books, is not engaged in rendering legal, financial, or professional services of any kind. If legal advice or other expert assistance is required, the reader is advised to seek the services of a competent professional.

Since 1917, Forbes has remained steadfast in its mission to serve as the defining voice of entrepreneurial capitalism. Forbes Books, launched in 2016 through a partnership with Advantage Media, furthers that aim by helping business and thought leaders bring their stories, passion, and knowledge to the forefront in custom books. Opinions expressed by Forbes Books authors are their own. To be considered for publication, please visit **books.Forbes.com**.

To Barbara, who has constantly brought out the very best in me and has never stopped believing in me. My partner in all things, and the love of my life.

THE BIZZICS WAY

CONTENTS

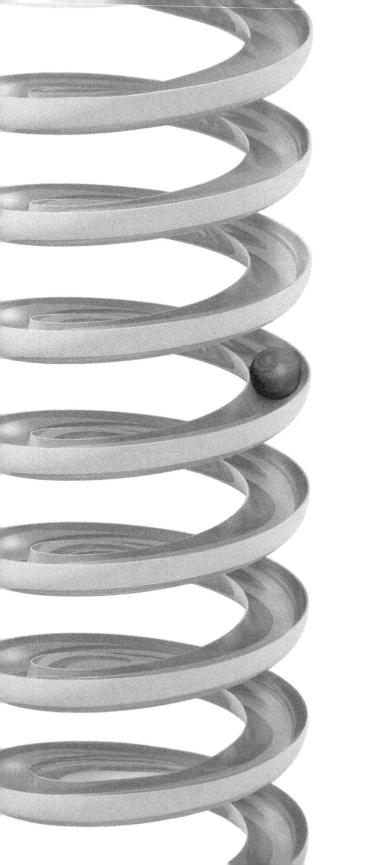

ACKNOWLEDGMENTS

I am filled with gratitude for so many who have made this dream a reality. For my parents, Joan and Bill Higgins, who gave me a chance in life and whose radical generosity gave me so many advantages that others do not have. For my siblings Peter, Sue, Marybeth, and Linda, who helped me understand that human bonds are the most powerful of all. For my children Chris, Kevin, and Laura, who helped me understand the boundless energy that comes with deep love. For Sister Rita Xavier and all the Sisters of Saint Joseph, who taught me the importance of core values and how to lead in order to serve. *Praesis ut Prosis*. For Marcus Mendenhall, who took the time for me when he had serious science to tend to. For Nick Miller, whose friendship and mentorship instilled in me that clarity and complete understanding are necessary to move forward on anything. For Deb Palmer George, who showed me the power of living and leading authentically. For Trey Holt, who inspired me to never quit on a dream and especially to not quit on myself—ever. For the entire Forbes Books team, who have brought excellence to every phase of this process and quite literally made my dream come true. For every employer who took a chance on me and helped me grow, and for those who did not and made me *want* to grow. And finally for my writing partner, Alison Kilian, whose extraordinary gifts made the conceptual tangible and whose friendship and encouragement got me to the finish line.

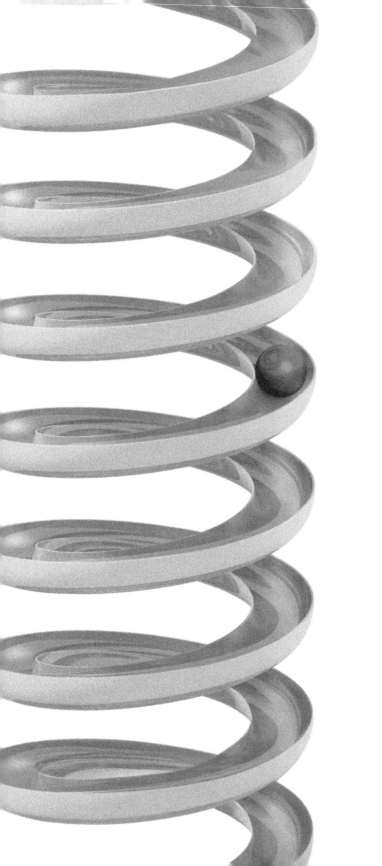

INTRODUCTION

W hat do you remember from your high school physics class? If you're like me, probably not much. Maybe you tried to forget high school altogether. Over four decades later, what I recall from my physics class most distinctly are energy, velocity, and momentum. Why?

Sister Rita Xavier.

Sister Rita taught physics at my alma mater, Bishop McGuinness High School, in Winston-Salem, North Carolina. Urban legend had it that she had worked with famed aerospace engineer Wernher von Braun in her early days. To us, she was a force of nature. She had a saying: "You be the door, and I'll slam you." We believed her!

While I was never a star physics student, Sister Rita certainly had my undivided attention. The three principles she taught us—energy, velocity, and momentum—have stayed with me my entire life, and they've grown in meaning and application over the years.

I've spent my career advising business owners at every stage, from start-up to expansion and acquisition. That work inspired me to delve into leadership and management topics. I've always been a curious person, and when I start to pull at a thread, I keep pulling. When I set out to learn more about leadership and management, I left no stone unturned. It would be difficult to list every leadership or management book I've read over the past forty years. I remember the first one: *Leadership Is an Art*, by Max De Pree. It remains one of my favorites. Since then, I've enjoyed thought leaders such as Jim Collins, Stephen M. R. Covey, John C. Maxwell, Patrick Lencioni, Seth Godin, and many others.

Through all that reading and learning, I had a persistent sense that there was something bigger, deeper, and more timeless and connected going on under the surface of their discussions of leadership and management.

Then, I started noticing those physics terms from my school days appearing in my work. Repeatedly, in discussions about business and leadership, words like *velocity, energy, momentum,* and *friction* appeared. I distinctly remember doing a leadership training and participating in a discussion about *momentum*. Everybody in the room was talking about business leadership, but, in my mind, I was back in that physics classroom in Winston-Salem. I could almost hear Sister Rita's voice talking about the law of momentum.

I soon realized that it wasn't a mere coincidence. It wasn't just that the terms were appearing across fields. In fact, the principles of physics could be applied to the business world. By looking to simple laws of nature, I could break down essential business best practices in a way that was accessible and understandable, and maybe even engaging, to everyone. It's taken years to refine this theory. This book is my mission to share it with small business owners like yourself.

I'm Not a Physicist, and You Don't Need to Be One Either

Like I said, I'm no physicist. I've spent the majority of my career—forty-plus years—in banking. Most people in the banking industry ended up in it by accident or fell into it because they had family in the field. That wasn't the case for me; I consciously chose to be in banking. It's a decision I made way back in high school. Why?

I grew up in Winston-Salem, a big banking town. Banking powerhouse Wachovia was headquartered locally, while First Union was in nearby Charlotte. Now, I didn't come from a banking family—my father worked in textiles—but I knew many bankers, mostly neighbors and parents of friends. What struck me about them was the important role they played in the community. It wasn't so much the financial part of the job that resonated with me. It was the way the bankers I knew contributed to the neighborhood and built it up.

Back then, before online banking was a thing, the bank was a community hub. People didn't just go there for money. It was a relational place. If you were a kid stopping by to open your first savings account with ten dollars in your hand, people would take the time to congratulate you and celebrate you. It was an encouraging place.

There was just something about the energy and the psyche of a small business owner that made my day.

So, I set off for college with an eye on banking. I graduated from the University of North Carolina at Chapel Hill with a bachelor's degree in economics. I remember telling a former teacher of mine I was majoring in econ, and their response was, "Oh, how dreary!" In a way, they were right. But I had my sights set on something bigger than the formulas and calculus of economics. After graduation, I joined the management training program at First American National Bank in Nashville—in pursuit of my banking dream.

That's where I discovered my passion for working with entrepreneurs. There was just something about the energy and the psyche of a small business owner that made my day. When somebody came in and told me that they were getting ready to start or grow their business and they were looking for a lender, it always captured my imagination. I thought, *This is something these people really want to do, and they've got this level of self-confidence about it that's really inspiring.*

I've worked with many different types of business owners across all fields, and they all shared that entrepreneurial drive. One of the earlier clients I advised had an entire business around coin-operated video game machines like PAC-MAN, Pole Position, Super Mario Bros., Asteroids, Space Invaders, and Donkey Kong. He was constantly finding new places to put in machines, say in a diner or a bar (high-traffic areas). Then, he'd get the capital from the bank to purchase and install the machine. It was a very straightforward business model. At the time, it worked very well.

I've worked with thousands of small business owners like that one. I use the term *small* business as a conversational convenience. The US Small Business Administration (SBA) defines a firm with fewer than five hundred employees as "small."[1] To me, a small business can be as small as a solopreneur, like the gentleman described above pursuing the American dream of large-scale success. However, I do not believe that dreams are a relative matter. Just because a business is defined as "small" does not mean its dreams are small. Who knows how big a dream can be and how big any business can become in pursuing that dream?

I've also worked with companies at the other end of the spectrum—businesses that are by no definition, mine or the SBA's, "small." An example would be a relationship I had with Kinko's, an old copy-and-print chain. It was the mid-1990s. The founder of Kinko's had built a fortune replicating his business model across the

---

1   "Size Standards," US Small Business Administration, June 21, 2023, https://www.sba. gov/federal-contracting/contracting-guide/size-standards.

US. Instead of franchising his idea, he built business partnerships with operators in nearly every state. I met the Kinko's business partner in Tennessee, as the bank I was working for had helped him set up about ten stores across the state. He started as an employee in the Knoxville store and worked hard to maximize the opportunity, until he was owning stores himself.

That was the kind of partner the Kinko's founder wanted to work with, state to state. And partnering with those kinds of entrepreneurial individuals proved successful. Kinko's never went public, but FedEx bought it for $2.2 billion.[2] After that, you'd see FedEx-Kinko's cobranded stores.[3] Now, they're solely FedEx branded. That kind of enterprise deal showed me what was possible when a small independent business scaled up. Kinko's went from a one-man show to a billion-dollar enterprise.

In any case, regardless of the size of the business, I always admired the spirit of the entrepreneurs I worked with. However, I saw that they were often underserved and lacked the resources needed to make a quantum leap of progress—and I became determined to change that.

Tackling the Resource Gap: Helping Small Business Owners Make the Quantum Leap

I left the banking industry briefly to earn my master of business administration at UNC's Kenan-Flagler Business School. When I

---

2   Rick Brooks, "FedEx to Buy Kinko's for $2.2 Billion," *Wall Street Journal*, December 31, 2003, https://www.wsj.com/articles/SB107278969871498900.

3   Alana Semuels, "Kinko's Founder All Shook Up as FedEx Drops the K-name," *Los Angeles Times*, June 15, 2008, https://www.latimes.com/archives/blogs/money-company/story/2008-06-15/kinkos-founder-all-shook-up-as-fedex-drops-the-k-name.

returned to banking, my MBA equipped me to deal exclusively with commercial clients of all sizes. However, my unique interest in entrepreneurs never faded. As luck would have it, First American—the bank I was working for at the time—expanded its focus on small businesses. As part of that expansion, I moved into a strategic role.

My new position allowed me to combine my MBA training with ten-plus years of practical banking experience to help business owners at all levels. The role demanded a highly strategic level of analysis. If the bank issued a loan to a business owner, we wanted them to succeed. My job was to figure out how to make that happen. I was essentially responsible for figuring out how the bank was deploying to help business owners. What did the resource allocation look like? How was the bank itself organizing to meet businesses' needs?

That's when I started to notice a gap. At one end, there were large corporate clients, massive revenue generators that had the money needed to tap into whatever business resources they desired. At the other end was this mass of small businesses that didn't have access to those tools. They weren't "big enough" to get the best financial advisors, top-tier coaches, or elite consultants. They couldn't pay thousands for business or leadership guidance.

As a result, these individuals often lacked the ability to make the leap. The concept of the quantum leap has made its way beyond physics; we now know it colloquially as a big increase or jump forward—a form of progress, often abrupt. Small business owners often can't make these kinds of leaps because they don't have the right resources. I saw that these people needed an advocate, and I wanted to be that person—the professional working inside the bank who could connect these individuals with the best resources possible.

As I took on that role, my job expanded way beyond banking and money matters. Yes, financial capital is necessary for businesses to survive. Securing capital is important. However, many business owners are left to their own devices after they secure that capital. They're left in a vacuum. Seeing this, I became very intentional about serving those business owners' needs—and that's been my mission ever since.

I'd say that's been the sweet spot in my career: I learned what customers needed from a bank, beyond money, and figured out how to strategically deploy bank resources accordingly. Banks I've worked for have been recognized nationally as high performing by Greenwich Associates, the most highly respected commercial banking research firm in the nation. In 2017, my then-employer tied for the most Small Business Excellence awards among thousands of banks in the survey universe.[4] These accolades showed me that my efforts to help small business owners were working. It felt good—but I also felt like I could do more.

Coaching 101: Getting Small Business Owners Greater Guidance

While I was discovering my passion for helping business owners, I was also developing my own career. As I advanced to executive leadership positions in the banking industry, I learned how to effectively lead a team. I wasn't just a banker issuing a loan. I was a leader who had to communicate, motivate, and inspire others, so we could best serve our clients.

---

4   "Superior Client Ratings Propel Pinnacle to Win 30 Greenwich Excellence Awards," *Pinnacle Financial Partners*, February 7, 2018, https://www.pnfp.com/about-pinnacle/media-room/news-releases/superior-client-ratings-propel-pinnacle-to-win-30-greenwich-excellence-awards.

That executive experience presented fresh challenges and gave me renewed empathy for the business owners I worked with. I was at the helm throughout organizational changes and restructuring, and grappled with issues every leader faces at some point, like maintaining the appropriate levels of energy and excitement in a team. In a way, I felt like I was my own small business owner, managing my people so they could deliver their best every day.

I was fortunate to work for organizations that supported my leadership development. I had access to excellent resources, including coaches who helped me improve my own leadership style. My own good fortune had me coming back to that gap I'd noticed previously: *I* had access to these resources. What about those that didn't? That's when I started exploring coaching.

I'd been meeting with a mentor for about a year when he said, "I'd like to do this video series with you on John C. Maxwell's *21 Irrefutable Laws of Leadership*." I agreed, and he took me through the book—and I found it extremely rewarding. It made a lot of vague concepts around leadership very tangible. For example, one of John's teachings is to always add value to others or, as he puts it, "Be a river, not a reservoir."

Through this work, I identified areas where I could improve as a leader. I soon noticed a difference in how I was leading—and in how people were responding. So, I started implementing John's teachings at work. I had a team of about eight people at the time, and I wasn't sure how they would react. They loved it. That's when I thought, *I should do this more often.*

In 2011, I became a founding member of the John C. Maxwell team of certified coaches, speakers, and trainers. Becoming part of the coaching team gave me the opportunity to teach and help other people improve their own leadership abilities. Especially in smaller businesses, leadership influences everything. If you have the right leader, it's a critical difference-maker. So, my involvement in coaching was largely driven by my mission to help entrepreneurs.

Since then, I've had the opportunity to work as a leadership coach in all kinds of contexts, from the business community in my hometown of Nashville to a school in Uganda (a wonderful experience I'll discuss more in chapters 4 and 5).

The more coaching I did, the more I began to wonder: Why do small business owners not use these kinds of resources? I started talking to the small business owners I knew and learned that money was a major barrier. Many coaches charge $1,000 per month or more. For a new entrepreneur, that's cash they just cannot afford to spend.

Bizzics: An Accessible Resource for Entrepreneurs

The right resources and coaching can be game-changing for small business owners. But I don't want people to feel like they've got to go to an executive program at Harvard to learn leadership skills. That's why I developed Bizzics.

I mentioned how I kept seeing those physics terms, haunting me from my days as a student with Sister Rita Xavier, pop up in my adult life. As a banker advising businesses, as an executive honing my own leadership skills, and as a coach—again and again—I noticed those concepts jumping out at me: *energy, velocity, momentum,* and so forth.

I took those ideas and, with the help of physicist Marcus Mendenhall, explored how they might apply to the business world. Marcus has a PhD in physics from the California Institute of Technology. We met through our kids; my oldest son was in the same Boy Scout troop as his son, and I could tell right away that Marcus was brilliant.

Whenever there was a troop challenge, like building a trebuchet, Marcus drove the whole project, and we always won.

So, when I started thinking about how the laws of physics might be applied to business, I reached out to Marcus. It had been at least ten years since I had seen him, but he graciously agreed to talk to me about my ideas of how physics might apply to business. We set up a series of interviews and spoke for hours. Those podcasts, the foundation of Bizzics, are still on the Bizzics website today.

As a scientist, Marcus warned me against oversimplifying analogies: of course, the laws of physics don't hold up 100 percent in the business world. Yet the simplicity and elegance of these natural principles align with best business practices because they both rest on the fulcrum of energy. Nothing happens without it. And we in the business world are all about energy.

In 2019, I founded Bizzics. Now, I'm sharing the Bizzics principles with you. I feel a sense of urgency sharing this information, for a few reasons. There are 33.2 million "small" businesses in the United States.[56] Those small businesses employ some 46.4 percent of the private workforce in the country. They're impacting everyday lives. Many of those businesses also suffered greatly during the COVID-19 pandemic, which disproportionately affected smaller business owners. That's one reason I'm writing this book now.

I further feel compelled to write this book now because of some concern I have about where modern business owners are getting their information. In the past, I had confidence in the banking system as a

---

5   Emily Williams, "Advocacy Releases 2022, Small Business Profiles for the States and Territories," US Small Business Administration Office of Advocacy, August 31, 2022, https://advocacy.sba.gov/2022/08/31/advocacy-releases-2022-small-business-profiles-for-the-states-and-territories/.

6   "Size Standards," US Small Business Administration, June 21, 2023, https://www.sba.gov/federal-contracting/contracting-guide/size-standards.

place that people could get insights from bankers, experienced professionals who had seen dozens of businesses rise and fall, who would be able to give a new business owner solid advice and say, "Hey, I wouldn't do that if I were you" (or whatever feedback was warranted).

The system has become less personal and more mechanized. Everything is driven by technology; everything is online. When I started in banking in 1984, the US had over 14,000 commercial banks. At the time of this writing, there are roughly 4,200.[7] Fundamental economic principles impact every industry—it's the invisible hand of the marketplace, and I have learned to respect it. But I also must acknowledge the human capital lost and what it means to small business relationships.

I'm afraid that gap I already pinpointed will widen. Big companies will still have the money to get the best resources, coaches, and consultants, while small business owners will lack the funds to get that kind of help.

This also leads to a risk of small business owners trusting bad information. In the later stages of my career, I've noticed small business owners are trying to self-service advice by going online for information. However, there isn't a lot of curation or personalization as to what information might be good versus bad, or right for them. The risk of wrong information is great.

This brings me to another, very personal, part of my motivation to write this book. It's because I have seen, firsthand, the cost of people not making it. I want things to work out for people. Unfortunately, in the banking industry, not every story is a success story. I've seen people lose their savings. I've seen people lose their homes. It pains me to admit that I've had two customers take their own lives following

---

7   "BankFind Suite: Find Annual Historical Bank Data," Federal Deposit Insurance Corporation, 2021, https://banks.data.fdic.gov/explore/historical/.

financial problems resulting from failing businesses. Those individuals weigh on my mind to this day.

I hope that, by giving small business owners access to good ideas and good people, this kind of loss can be avoided. Not only that, I hope the path to entrepreneurship can be made a little easier—because it can get stony.

It's taken me nearly four decades of experience as a banker, executive leader, and coach to develop the Bizzics principles. Perhaps the seed was planted when I was sitting in Sister Rita Xavier's classroom as a kid (and hoping she wouldn't call on me). Throughout my career, I've seen how hard it is for business owners to get the assistance they need to lead with confidence. If I can communicate some clear, concise ideas to a business owner—like yourself—and help them make the leap, there's a lot of power in that.

I mentioned how I've always been sort of enamored by the entre-preneurial spirit and admired people who have the guts to start their own business. The entrepreneurs I've worked with have made my career an exciting and fulfilling journey. With this book, I hope I can give something back to that community.

It's Not Rocket Science

You don't have to be a physicist to get value out of this book. You don't even have to *like* physics. But if you're looking for step-by-step, practical guidance for starting, growing, and leading your own business, this book can serve you.

My intention is to guide you to the holy grail of any organization: momentum. Momentum is one of those things that is readily recognized and highly desirable to most. However, it's often not understood in its full depth—which makes it impossible to intentionally build and sustain. This book gets under the surface of the canon of business and leadership advice to clearly carve out a path small business owners can take to achieve consistent momentum.

Each of the following chapters is based on one essential physics concept. I'll introduce the physics term, explain how that scientific principle relates to the business world, and provide anecdotes and case studies for clarity. We'll look at everything from how to energize teams to how to deliberately control growth. At the end of each chapter,

I'll direct you to resources that put that chapter's ideas into action—templates, checklists, and other tools to guide business and leadership development.

My conclusions are based on over forty years of experience working with small business owners and on a lot my own reading, coaching, and exploration. I invite you to test these concepts out and put them into practice in your "lab"—your own business. I've presented you with the hypothesis. Now, let's get on to building and sustaining momentum in your business.

THE BIZZICS WAY

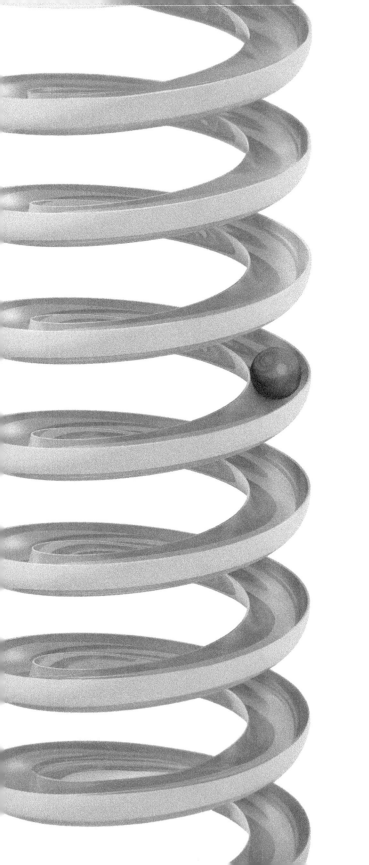

CHAPTER 1

Energy

Before we can start talking about momentum, we need to take a deep dive on energy, especially in a business context. Nothing happens in this world—or in business—without energy. The conservation of energy principle states that energy is neither created nor destroyed. It exists in a steady state, and the total energy remains constant. But there are different types of energy: kinetic and potential.

One way to explain it is to picture a ball sitting on a tabletop. That ball, even when it's not moving, has potential energy stored in it. Now, if you give that ball a nudge, and it starts rolling, that potential energy becomes kinetic energy.

This is where things get interesting for a businessperson. Think of all those times you've felt "stuck," a favorite coaching term—for example, in a work project. It's not that you can't get the job done. You can. What if you could take that potential energy and transform it into kinetic energy—get the ball rolling, so to speak? How do you *get going*?

This ability to tap into potential energy and transform it to kinetic energy is even more important if you're starting your own business. Even if you're just beginning to think about the business, you want to make sure you have the energy to not only get started but also to sustain and maintain the kinetic energy, the rolling ball, for weeks, months, years, maybe even *decades* to come. If you've got that energy, it can take you far. Do you?

> ## 🔑 KEY BUSINESS QUESTION:
>
> Where's the energy coming from in your business, and how can you transform that potential into power?

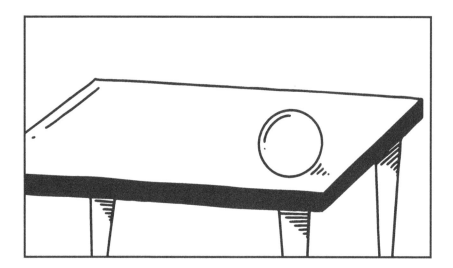

Do You Have Entrepreneurial Energy?

Over the course of my career, I became determined to do something completely different for business owners in the banking context. One way I did that was through "Masterminding," a concept I learned through the John C. Maxwell program. Masterminds date back to Napoleon Hill's 1937 work *Think and Grow Rich*, and John and his team have done great things with the model. Through Mastermind groups, John and his team bring together business leaders, offering them peer brainstorming, education, accountability, and support—and connecting them with resources.

While working for Pinnacle Financial Partners in Nashville, I decided to offer a Mastermind program for small business owners through the bank. Groups of seven or eight business owners would come in, and our bank officers would facilitate an eight-week Mastermind experience on the book *The E-Myth Revisited*, by Michael E. Gerber. It was such a success that we brought the initiative to all one hundred offices across the bank's footprint. I was responsible for visiting the various markets to help with the implementation.

This experience gave me the opportunity to gain insights into many struggles business owners face, and it helped highlight that gap I mentioned in the introduction. I noticed a hunger among entrepreneurs for business and leadership training, but not enough reliable resources available to them—which is a shame, because those skills are learnable.

The other commonality I noticed across the many Mastermind groups I worked with was that some participants inevitably realized they should have *never* gotten into business at all. In every group, some percentage of the population would decide that they'd started a business for the wrong reason and would subsequently close up shop. They realized they didn't have the necessary entrepreneurial energy.

I never considered these cases failures. When Pinnacle's Mastermind participants had those moments where they realized, essentially, "My heart is not in this," and they bowed out, I had no problem with that. Like I said in the introduction, I have seen people lose money, homes, families, and even their lives over businesses gone wrong. If you're going to start this journey, you've got to make sure you have the energy it will require. But where does that entrepreneurial energy come from?

Finding Your Power Source: How to Tap into Your Entrepreneurial Energy

Every object has energy stored in it. That's potential energy. If that object is put into motion, that potential energy transforms into kinetic energy. If the object stops its motion, it's back to potential energy. But the energy is always there, just taking different forms. That energy is in any object's molecular content.

An object is made up of molecules in constant motion—they vibrate. This vibration is the matter's energy; it can even be measured, as a temperature. The more energy an object has, the more the molecules are vibrating, and the higher the object's temperature. Even things we consider cold and inanimate have potential energy.

One of the most profound examples we have of energy creation is the sun. Hydrogen atoms at the core of the sun are in a violent vibrational field, banging into each other. This creates fusion, where the hydrogen turns into helium. That fusion is the most significant power source that we know. It's so strong that we have to live a long way from the sun to absorb its energy safely. Even then, we have to protect ourselves against it by staying in the shade or wearing sunscreen.

The sun clearly shows how molecular vibration has the potential to produce something very powerful. The question is, what does that high-vibrating energy look like for an entrepreneur—and do you have it? Like I said, not everybody does.

The E-Myth Revisited, by Michael E. Gerber, is a book I recommend to every small business owner. In his book, Gerber writes about the "entrepreneurial seizure." Basically, he says that most businesses are started by people who are in a situation they're trying to get away from. There's a convulsion to get out or away, for example from a bad boss, a toxic work environment, or an unfulfilling role.

The problem is this means starting your business on a negative note. That's low vibrational energy. It's not the kind of radiating, high-vibrating energy you find at the core of the sun. It's not the kind of energy that's capable of *transforming elements*. It's not the kind of energy that gets you jumping out of bed in the morning saying, **Low vibrational energy is simply not sustainable.** "Wow, I can't believe that I get to work on my business today!" It's the difference between running toward versus running away from something. The problem is that low vibrational energy is simply not sustainable.

When we're at our peak vibrational experience with the highest level of personal energy, we're experiencing things like joy, pleasure, and gratitude. For entrepreneurs, that typically aligns with chasing things that excite them, with the intention of helping people or solving a unique problem in an authentic way. It occurs when we bring the best of ourselves to others.

Endurance athlete and speaker Rich Roll puts it like this: "Service is the ultimate renewable energy source, like when you're coming from that place, from the heart where you're like, 'I'm really here to try to convey something that can be of benefit to other people.' That's what sees you through the adversity. That's what's going to allow you to show up for it day after day when you're facing obstacles."[8]

Think of entrepreneurs who made it big. They were likely operating in that high-energy field that seeks to serve others. Sara Blakely of SPANX is a favorite example of mine. She had a product she truly believed in and that she thought could help women feel great. With persistence, she got herself a ten-minute meeting to pitch her flagship product—footless body-shaping pantyhose—to an executive at Neiman Marcus department stores.

According to Sara's own account, the pitch didn't go well. So, she cut it short and asked the (female) executive to join her in the bathroom, so she could demonstrate her product in action. On the spot, Sara modeled her outfit, a pair of white pants, with and without SPANX.[9] The executive was sold. There's still a photo of that check from Neiman Marcus, one of Sara's first major orders, on the SPANX website.[10]

That's the kind of high-vibrational energy that will make your business go the distance. It is that firm belief in a vision of helping people, most of whom you will never meet. You will do the awkward, unthinkable, courageous thing every time to help them. How do you get the guts to do it?

The vibrational energy for a small business owner comes from the gap between where they are today and where they envision their business being in the future. When people bounce back and forth

---

8   Rich Roll, "Service Is the Ultimate Energy Source," May 19, 2023, 0:00 to 0:52, YouTube video, https://www.youtube.com/watch?v=chuQwl9otk8.

9   Julia La Roche, "How Billionaire Sara Blakely Pitched SPANX to Neiman Marcus in a Bathroom," Yahoo! Finance, February 14, 2018, https://finance.yahoo.com/news/billionaire-sara-blakely-incredible-story-got-spanx-neiman-marcus-235743342.html.

10 "About Us," *SPANX*, n.d., accessed September 25, 2023, https://spanx.com/pages/about-us.

between their current state and a goal they want to achieve, that creates a powerful vibrational field. It creates tremendous energy and heat—the kind that fueled Sara. Sara wanted to see SPANX in every major department store in the US, a clear sign that thousands of people had benefited from her unique solution. That's what kept her motivated.

If you want to get that entrepreneurial energy, you've got to start by defining your goals—or, more broadly, articulating your vision. That vision could be achieving a certain financial objective or successfully helping your target audience or penetrating a specific market.

Consider your motivation. Who is it you're trying to help? What are you offering? Where do you want to be? One coach of mine used an approach called appreciative inquiry, which is all about self-determined change: Considering who you are, and knowing all the different things you know about yourself, what is the logical outcome? What do you desire?

The more tangible you can make your objective, the better. If your vision is vague and lacking definition, it will be difficult to create a high-energy vibration because there is nothing concrete to bounce off of.

Vision boards are a great example of how you can take a muddy objective and give it clarity. Another way to crystallize that vision is to ask yourself this question (a coaching favorite): If you knew you couldn't fail and you had every resource you needed at your disposal, what would your moment of greatest success look like? Now put that on your vision board.

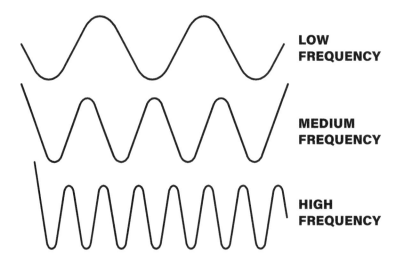

LOW FREQUENCY

MEDIUM FREQUENCY

HIGH FREQUENCY

⚗ TO THE LAB!

I've included some resources to help you assess your energy as an entrepreneur in the "In Your Lab" resource section at the conclusion of chapter 1. See the Energy Health Check.

When you feel your energy flagging, you can come back to that vision board. That's what will keep your energy going. You'll be constantly attracted and reattracted to your goal and keep bouncing back and forth between the "where I am" versus the "where I want to be." It's how you'll keep your entrepreneurial molecules buzzing and energized.

Building Out Your Power Grid: Share Your Vision to Energize Those around You

I hope your vision is so audacious that there is no possible way for you to achieve it on your own. Even if you start as a solopreneur, odds are that it will not always stay that way. Whenever there is more than one stakeholder, you have to consider energy distribution. As you begin to move, your kinetic energy must be captured and transferred to others, like partners, employees, suppliers, and customers.

That is how energy fundamentally works. Whether thermal, wind, water, or solar, highly charged particles on the move are captured and transformed by a turbine or similar mechanism into usable electricity. Think of the Hoover Dam, where you've got water moving at fierce velocity. It generates about four billion kilowatt-hours of hydroelectric power each year, serving more than one million people in Nevada, Arizona, and California.[11]

It is *your* job to build out your own power grid and pass on your entrepreneurial energy to other stakeholders. You must master communications of all types, including written and spoken words, visual representations, and even the actions you take. In Sara Blakely's case, she literally showed the buyer her product in the department store bathroom to communicate her product's value.

Are you starting to get a sense of why your entrepreneurial energy must be abundant? You don't want to be without energy in business. Have you ever spent an extended period of time without power? Maybe you were hit by an ice storm? Tornado? Hurricane? Brownout? Whatever the cause, some unwanted force disrupted the

---

11 "Hoover Dam," Bureau of Reclamation, n.d., accessed September 25, 2023, https://www.usbr.gov/lc/hooverdam/faqs/powerfaq.html.

flow of energy through the grid—or even took the grid down completely. It happens in business too.

I've seen the fallout of ignoring a business's energy and failing to sustain a functional power grid. A firm I worked for in my banking career underwent a major organizational change that resulted in some internal fractures. Basically, they acquired several companies and then failed to merge those companies' diverse cultures. They were so worried about the financial and operational side of things that they ignored the cultural side. So, people weren't really coalescing around a cohesive vision. The result? Distrust that broke the grid.

It got so bad they had to bring in a consultant. The consultant pinpointed the issue on day one: the organizational energy was off. So, they introduced a "mood elevator." At the top were attributes like *grateful, wise,* and *creative,* and in the basement were attributes like *angry, hostile,* and *depressed.* The ground floor was being *curious* and *interested,* a kind of neutral position. The cultural goal became for everyone to get the corporate energy, the mood elevator, off the ground floor and up to the higher tiers of positive energy, staying out of the basement at all costs. We had to rebuild the energy grid, which took well over a year. Some might argue that it was never fixed.

While that is a "large company" example, the lesson is the same for the small business owner. *You* are responsible for the constant flow of energy in your business, and it starts with your own high-voltage energy source. It needs to be a daily habit to avoid that powerlessness that leaves you at the mercy of all kinds of unwelcome forces.

The idea of being an energy distributor may exhaust you. I hope not. I hope it is simply a reality check. Because I have good news too: one of the distinct differences between physics and organizational leadership is that every person to whom you deliver *your* energy is also a potential energy producer in their own right. Each individual creates their own vibrational field as they come to see themselves incorporated into your business vision. The result? More molecules vibrating against that powerful vision of yours.

It has been shown that, when different things vibrate in close proximity to one another, they often synchronize and start to vibrate together at the same frequency. From neurons firing in the brain to fireflies flashing in sync, these moments of self-organization can be found everywhere in the natural world.[12] If you can harness that energy and get others vibrating in sync with you—what a lot of energy that will create!

Even better, each person on your team already has their own vibrational energy, distinct from your business. This is *their* gap between where they are in life and where they want to be. Each one comes to you as a whole person, seeking to know what they can become in the process of being on the journey with you. What does this association mean to them professionally? Financially? What does it mean to their family? How will they become a better person through living the values of your company?

When you can tap into each individual's personal energy, and integrate it into your own business vision, you have *really* built some energy in your business. But figuring out each person's vibrational energy requires some effort. Everybody is their own element. Leaders need to know their own strengths and weaknesses to navigate how to best lead all those diverse characters and get the overall organizational energy where it needs to be. This also helps to build a stronger organization—one with greater mass that's better able to withstand the blows of external forces.

---

12   Tam Hunt, "The Hippies Were Right: It's All about Vibrations, Man!," *Scientific American*, December 5, 2018, https://blogs.scientificamerican.com/observations/the-hippies-were-right-its-all-about-vibrations-man/.

Before leaders can draw out the strengths of others to build that mass, though, they've got to build their own strengths (which also means identifying weaknesses). Tools I've benefited from in that regard include the Myers-Briggs personality test and Gallup's StrengthsFinder (now CliftonStrengths). Enneagram personality typing is another useful tool. It's just about figuring out your inner self: How am I made up, and what am I cut out for? Knowing yourself is the first step to leading well.

With that self-awareness, it will become possible for you to take others on a similar inward journey where they discover their strengths, purpose, and passion. You can then build an awareness of how all can be served in the journey you propose. That's what your job is as a leader.

> ## 🧪 TO THE LAB!
>
> I've included some resources to help you understand your own strengths and weaknesses as a leader—and those of your employees—in the "In Your Lab" resource section at the conclusion of chapter 1. See the Personal Growth Plan.

Leadership and coaching have a lot in common. The main purpose of coaching is releasing human potential. It's finding out the *why* of people, the burning desire that drives them, and figuring out where they want to go. Leadership is similarly about energizing people. Even if you're a solopreneur, you've got to energize yourself. You've got to create a system that upholds those vibrations that create high energy, both within yourself and others. Those are the vibrations that will help sustain kinetic energy and keep you, your team, and your business moving.

Ensuring a Steady Power Source: How to Craft Culture

People will come and go at your company. You can't fully control those shifts in your power grid. The one thing you *can* control in your power grid is your culture. To me, culture *is* the grid. And culture is defined by the core values of the company.

Culture is something that a lot of small business owners don't consider. In the early days of entrepreneurship, they're focused on nuts and bolts like financing. They aren't necessarily considering culture. I've seen this backfire on organizations more than once, and I always advise on figuring out your business's culture at the start.

This matters even if you're a solopreneur or a very small business of just a couple of people. For one thing, defining your values when it's just two people is a lot easier than when it's twenty-five. And your culture is also relevant to your customers. It can attract or repel them. So, even solopreneurs should carefully consider the culture they want to embody. I promise you that it is very expensive to repair your grid, so take the time to get it right on the front end and carefully maintain it.

How do you define your culture? You can start by identifying your values. It's very important for small business owners to think about their value system, because the core values of an enterprise set the energetic frequency. As you grow your team, clear values will help you attract the right employees—those who share your values. And those shared values will then produce the highest level of energy in your people.

I've found a lot of smaller companies will try to do something memorable, like taking a word or the company name and using it to create an acronym that describes their business. But they don't take the time to sit down and reflect on their values in a meaningful way.

Partnership. Gratitude. Health. What are your values? Write them down. What do they look like in practice? Write that down.

You also want to consider your mission. This isn't your personal mission, but your business mission. What does your business hope to achieve in the bigger picture, beyond yourself? Defining your values and mission will help you shape your culture.

🧪 TO THE LAB!

I've included some resources to help you define your values and mission in the "In Your Lab" resource section at the conclusion of chapter 1. See the Mission Statement Template.

Now, I've also seen wonderful examples of culture done right. One is Pinnacle Financial Partners, where I worked for about eight years. When they began in 2000, the firm had three principal partners. Those three individuals sat down and established their values and mission before they ever opened up the bank. And that early attentiveness to values and mission has helped grow the organization dependably from three people to some 3,200. How so?

One of their big goals was that they wanted to be a great place to work, and they wanted a culture that reinforced that. Values they defined included points like integrity, partnership, and fairness. Every employee was educated on the core cultural values as part of their orientation, and those values framed each employee's performance review, regardless of seniority.

When it was time for performance reviews, everybody would have a "values report" as part of their review. Those reports would be submitted to the values committee, a group of about eight people, who then reviewed the values report and determined whether the person met the organization's values criteria or not. Each person was reviewed in the same way by the same committee, not just by their direct supervisor. If someone wasn't meeting a certain cultural objective, that became part of their development plan.

That's how you create an effective culture that has meaning and impact. And it all started with three people sitting down and saying to each other, "Hey, what are our values? What's our mission? What's important to us, and our future employees and customers?" Take the time to do that now and you'll avoid "power outages"—no energy left—later.

Harnessing Energy for Velocity

By being honest and vulnerable about the *why* of your business, you can help determine if you've got the energy needed for entrepreneurship. You've *got* to take the time to do that, because you don't want to be on a journey that you're not suited for. You want to start with the highest level of energy possible, because it only gets harder as you go along.

Also—coming back to our laws of physics—energy is what will give your business velocity. The momentum of any object is its mass times its velocity. Now, energy and velocity have a relationship that isn't linear but geometric. If you aren't a physicist yourself, you may be a little surprised by the relationship between velocity and energy. The rela-

By being honest and vulnerable about the *why* of your business, you can help determine if you've got the energy needed for entrepreneurship.

tionship between velocity and energy isn't one to one; rather, for velocity to double, energy has to *quadruple.*

Let's say your business is a car. If you're driving a car and want to increase your speed from fifty miles per hour to one hundred miles per hour, you want the largest engine possible—because you need four times the energy to reach that velocity. A Mercedes-Benz would be preferable to a Toyota Prius, because the engine is larger and more capable of an energy boost of that magnitude. That's what you want for your business.

If you get that energy component right and distribute that energy effectively, you'll be more likely to point your business in the right direction—and then gain the velocity you need to cover distance quickly and *grow.*

How do you get the velocity you need to achieve great growth—and how do you harness that velocity in a productive way? It's all about setting the right direction of your velocity vector and then controlling its speed. That's what I'll talk about in chapter 2, which is all about velocity—the next law of physics we're going to test out.

🧪 IN YOUR LAB

At the start of this chapter, I asked you where the energy in your business is coming from and how you can transform that potential into power. The Bizzics website has some resources to help you transform your potential energy to kinetic energy:

- **Energy Health Check:** Do you have the entrepreneurial energy needed to start a business?

- **Personal Growth Plan:** What are your personal goals—or your employees'?

- **Mission Statement Template:** What is your business going to achieve?

Velocity

A ll speed and no control. For businesses, this is a big sticking point. You don't want to just be going full steam ahead. You want to make sure that you're moving ahead in a direction you actually want to be going in, with a specific goal or destination in mind (distance), over a specific period of time (speed). The physics definition of velocity requires all three: direction, distance, and speed.

When I spoke to my physicist friend Marcus about velocity in business, he said that he would need to know a lot more about *direction* in business before he could offer an opinion on velocity in the business context. It's an important question, because half the equation for momentum (our ultimate goal for this book) is velocity. The other half is mass.

I loved the challenge of Marcus's question, because it may be the most underappreciated momentum factor for business—if the formula holds true. Most business owners I know are full of energy, but the clarity of direction has many shades and variations—so much so that that the direction becomes obscured and isn't clear at all.

When you're starting your business, you're focusing on that first step of nudging that stationary ball off the table and transforming your potential energy into kinetic energy. You're truly trying to "get the ball rolling." Getting that object in motion is only half the battle.

The question is, what direction do you want to take your business in? And how fast do you plan to go—or, in the business sense, grow?

Just as important is the need to determine the direction, distance, and speed of that motion. That's your velocity. The question is, what direction do you want to take your business in? And how fast do you plan to go—or, in the business sense, *grow*? Further, what direction will that growth take?

If you don't channel the energy and speed of your velocity in a linear direction, you risk your business getting stuck in place. I've seen it happen many times: entrepreneurs have some initial success and end up repeating the same actions that worked previously, without realizing that the context has changed. As a result, they fail to expand and end up spinning their wheels without moving an inch. The unfortunate thing is that they're still expending energy—often a great deal of energy—but they aren't moving in the direction they want to go in.

I like to compare it to a pinwheel firework. As a kid, I was a bit of a pyromaniac, and the community where I grew up was big on fireworks on the Fourth of July. Everybody would buy fireworks and set them off in their yards, their driveways, the street—any free space they could find. By the end of the night, the neighborhood would be enveloped in this kind of fog of war from all the spent fireworks. It felt like a movie scene. Today, that probably wouldn't be allowed—but back then, for a fire-loving kid like myself, it was a lot of fun.

A pinwheel firework is made of a powder-filled spiral tube with a pinwheel at the end. When ignited, the energy of the firework not only creates sparks and flames; it also causes the pinwheel to rotate, creating a burning, spinning circle. I remember that it made a spectacular display if you had it spinning around in your driveway—bright, hot, and full of motion. But it wouldn't *go* anywhere. It wasn't like a bottle rocket or a roman candle, which shot in a specific direction at a dramatic speed.

When I see a business owner lacking velocity, I think about that pinwheel firework. They might have a lot of energy and be creating a lot of heat and light—but they aren't going in any particular direction. There are a lot of businesses that get stuck in this cycle, for various reasons that I'll discuss.

When talking about velocity in business, there are two big points to consider. First, what direction do you want to go in? Second, how fast can you afford to go/grow? There are some frameworks and tools that can help you control velocity's direction and speed, which I'll get into.

> ## 🔑 KEY BUSINESS QUESTION:
>
> How fast are you going and where?

Where Is Your Business Going/Growing?

Instead of starting with the "how fast" of velocity, I want to talk about the "where." The *where* is all about direction. A lack of direction can lead to many pitfalls, from getting "stuck" to pursuing misplaced growth agendas.

In my banking career, I've seen how a lack of direction can result in an organization's downfall. In general, strategic direction is difficult in banking. There are very few banks that have grown organically in a way that allows them to expand meaningfully beyond a single community or state. Most of the time, they're stuck where they are. In some cases, they may end up acquiring another firm to grow. However, acquisition isn't always an ideal growth plan.

One of the most personally painful examples of this is the demise of Wachovia Bank. This was my hometown bank in Winston-Salem, North Carolina, and it became a banking powerhouse over a period of thirty years, expanding across broad geographies with an unrelenting discipline on credit quality. By 2008, it had grown to over $650 billion in assets by sticking to the basics that had made it great. It was the fourth-largest bank in the US, operating in twenty-one states and the District of Columbia.

While Wachovia experienced some other performance issues based on the size and complexity of some of the credits it underwrote, its acquisition of Golden West Financial in California in 2006 proved to be its downfall. The strategic acquisition and move to California itself was successful. However, in the process of the acquisition, Wachovia acquired roughly $122 billion in adjustable-rate home mortgages—a business area the bank had little experience with. Coming right at the cliff of the 2008 housing bust, it proved to be a disaster.

In the first quarter of 2007, Wachovia reported $2.3 billion in earnings. By the second quarter of 2008, the bank posted an $8.9 billion loss. By the end of 2008, Wachovia was acquired by Wells Fargo.[13]

The bank that largely inspired me to embark on a career in banking no longer exists. It all came down to an abandonment of the strategic direction that had made them a dominant banking firm for decades. I do not know anyone in banking who would have predicted that credit quality would be the downfall of Wachovia.

Those kinds of risky business decisions are unfortunately all too common when a business doesn't have a strong sense of strategic direction. What's more, that strategic direction needs to be supported by active *movement* in that direction; you can't just maintain operations and expect the business to move in that direction. How can you define that direction? Let's talk about some methods.

DEFINING YOUR BUSINESS DIRECTION: THREE PARTS OF A STRATEGIC FRAMEWORK

Every business owner I've talked to wants "more." However, often there isn't a lot of rigorous thought around what "more" means. What does it look like for your business? It could mean moving into a new market—expanding geographically, for example—or adding a new product or service. So, how will you define *your* business direction? There are a few things to think about.

---

13   Scott G. Alvarez, "The Acquisition of Wachovia Corporation by Wells Fargo & Company," Board of Governors of the Federal Reserve System, September 1, 2010, https://www.federalreserve.gov/newsevents/testimony/alvarez20100901a.htm.

Market Share

First, there is the very simple one-dimensional view of business. Think of your unique value proposition, USP. Whom does it serve? If you have thought through whom you want to serve with your USP, you will direct all your energy toward them. The desired direction is *up*, which means more market share. You get to decide how much market share and by when.

Picture it like this: a simple X/Y chart with market share on the vertical axis and time on the horizontal axis. You set a clear vector (direction and magnitude) and speed expressed in days, months, or years on the horizontal axis. You have all the components—speed, distance, direction—in front of you.

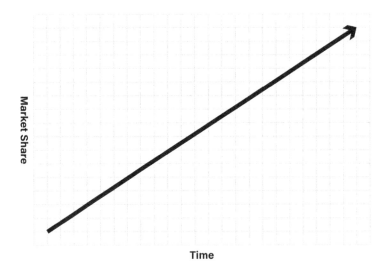

Market Share

Time

You might say, "Well, I'm just a small business. I don't have access to market share data. That's for big companies like Coca-Cola or Procter & Gamble." Like I said in the introduction, I don't really believe in "big" or "small" when it comes to businesses. The principles—the laws of nature or, in this case, of Bizzics—remain the same. You don't need a massive market share or complicated tools to calculate market share. It can be a lot simpler than that.

Here's an example of what I mean. I've lived in the same neighborhood for thirty years. I have done business with the same waste removal company that entire time. It's a very small family-owned business called Music City Disposal. I bet they have 80 percent market share in our neighborhood of over 450 homes. I see their trucks come through twice a week.

Whenever I see those trucks rolling through, I think about when that business was just starting out. It was the late 1970s, and our neighborhood, which is on the outskirts of Nashville, was just being built; before that, there was nothing here. It's safe to assume that Music City Disposal was very intentional in developing their business in this area at the time. It was a targeted neighborhood strategy that involved approaching one household at a time. That's an example of specific direction on market share—house by house, neighborhood by neighborhood. I don't know what time frame they set for themselves to corner the market here, but I'm confident they had an idea, or they wouldn't have the market share they have today.

Another example: I know of a company headquartered in Nashville called Southwestern/Great American, which employs hundreds of students every summer to sell educational books door to door in residential areas. It's commission work. I promise you, those young people know what kind of share they are getting out of each neighborhood they sell in. I know that the home office knows too. It's a summer job, so they've got about sixty days to capture X percent of the market. To me, that's another great example of velocity in relation to market share.

You can do the same if you know the markets and demographics you intend to serve. I like market share as a means of defining velocity, because it is tightly wound around your business intention—and it logically leads to revenue. Some companies may focus on revenue itself. Others may point to units sold over a particular share. Each of those options may dilute your strategic focus, as you find yourself doing anything for money (opportunity costs) or selling to people who are less likely to be wowed by your unique solution. Market share focuses on the market—who you're serving—and brings you back to your USP, which is how you're benefiting who you're serving.

Client Retention

No single measurement can ensure your success. The best businesses to me are the ones that acknowledge the complexity of business when they set their direction. Market share naturally leads to a discussion of client satisfaction and retention—because you want to ideally move into markets where there is clientele. Client satisfaction should be prominent in your direction as well because, presumably, you're in this for the long haul. You could grow market share rapidly but have poor client retention because your client satisfaction is low. That won't be sustainable.

So, if we add client retention to the conversation, we now move from one dimension to two, creating a four-quadrant grid. Market share stays on the vertical axis, and client satisfaction rests on the horizontal access. You can scale it from low to high (say, one to ten) or use whatever scaling measure you like. The point is that you are now solving for two things simultaneously. Pick a spot where you want to be. Most people I know would pick the upper-right quadrant—high market share, high satisfaction. Plot where you are today and draw that vector and pick your time frame to get there. That is velocity. You may be surprised at how quickly you can move once you've defined it all.

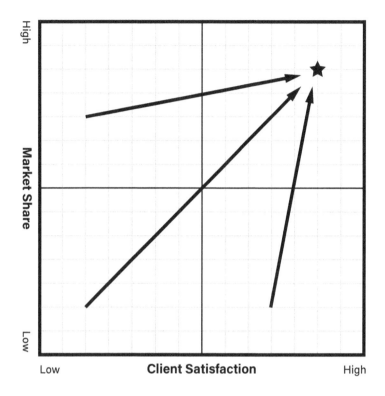

You never want to scale up at the expense of customer satisfaction. Customer satisfaction is paramount. One fantastic example of a business owner who's really understood this is Paul Orfalea, founder of the copy chain Kinko's. He got his start while he was still a student at the University of Southern California, Santa Barbara (UCSB). He rented one Xerox copier and an offset printer and set up shop in a leased space near campus.

He also sold stationery, pens, pencils, and basic school supplies—things students and professors would need.

Orfalea was catering to a demanding market. He was dealing

You never want to scale up at the expense of customer satisfaction.

with students who needed their course packs and wanted to make the grade, and with professors who needed their materials done *just so*. Given that audience, customer service was an important component of Orfalea's offering. At the start, he was running the copier and printer himself; later, he developed a self-service model, which cut down on waiting times and kept people happy—since many of his customers had deadlines to beat.

From the very start of Orfalea's business, the quality had to be outstanding. He delivered. Then, with time, he was able to expand. However, that expansion was highly strategic. Orfalea focused primarily on college towns where he knew there was a need. He always had his end customer in mind, and he always prioritized quality.[14] The fact that Orfalea's brainchild was ultimately acquired by FedEx—a company that defines high performance on the basis of speed and reliability, in their case of package delivery—really seems meant to be.

Profitability

There is a third dimension that needs to be honored for the longevity and ultimate value of your business—profitability. If not done wisely, rapid market share gains and high client satisfaction levels can actually have a negative profitability impact. You *may* have deep enough pockets to buy market share, scale operations rapidly, and deliver good service to your clients—but most business owners face a reality check when it comes to meeting these demands.

Imagine a third axis that scales according to a profitability metric in your industry, such as after-tax profit levels. You're now operating in a three-dimensional world that encompasses the effectiveness and sustainability of your business model. Instead of a top-right quadrant, you're aimed at the back-right corner—highest market share, highest client satisfaction, and highest profitability in your industry. That is a valuable combination. Again, pick the spot where you want to be, mark where you are, and pick a time frame to get there. That is velocity.

---

14 Encyclopedia.com, s.v. "Kinko's Incorporated," accessed September 25, 2023, https://www.encyclopedia.com/economics/economics-magazines/kinkos-incorporated.

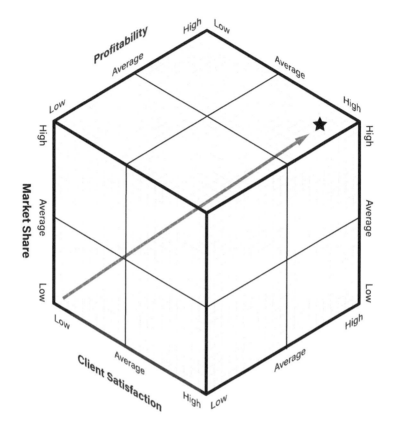

That may seem like a lot, but I promise that the most success-ful companies think this way. Years ago, I worked for a company whose CEO was notorious for setting challenging goals in every facet of business. Some of the goals were seemingly at odds with each other. Sometimes, his employees would ask, "Which one is the most important?" Without blinking, he would reply, "They are *all* important." He was right. That is the complexity of the business world.

In my experience, companies usually don't incorporate this third dimension into their way of thinking soon enough. The pro-gression I usually see goes something like this: a business owner has launched their company and has a lot of expenses to cover; they're passionately trying to get the clients that will create revenue to cover those expenses; they then realize how expensive and exhausting it is to always find *new* clients and start dreaming of securing returning clients. *This* is when they start to get serious about client satisfaction and product/service quality—too late. The approach is basically the opposite of Paul Orfalea's.

The problem is that it can be very expensive to provide top-quality client service that creates such a high level of satisfaction that people are guaranteed to return. So, the business* owner starts running into cash flow issues. And *this* is when the business owner starts to think more seriously about profitability. From what I've seen in my experiences with small business owners, it may be too late at that point.

You've got to be serious about your profit plan from day one. It's an essential part of your planning process. You can start by researching what profitability levels are standard for others in your industry. Then you've got to set informed goals for your own profitability. This allows you to (for example) communicate to investors, "This is where we're headed. What we're trying to do is get to 5 percent after tax, while having high market share and providing a great service." You can point at your cube, like the one above, and show exactly where the dot is that's balancing market share, client retention, and profitability.

How Fast Is Your Business Going/Growing?

Now, there's another aspect to velocity besides direction: speed. It's important to ask yourself, repeatedly, "What is the appropriate speed for my growth?" You've got to decide not only where you want to go but also how quickly you want to get there. While you don't want to get stuck, you also don't want to fall victim to hypergrowth.

There's some sensationalism around entrepreneurship that raises the risk of hypergrowth. Especially in the US, with its notorious start-up scene of Silicon Valley as a backdrop, there's a capitalistic urge to make it big, *fast*. People champion big funding initiatives that allow for a fortune to be amassed quickly—but those seemingly "overnight" success stories (rarely, in fact, overnight) may struggle to maintain equilibrium.

Some companies plan for hypergrowth by making big capital raises; pursuing large-scale, high-quality hires (sometimes even over-hiring); contracting out production; or selecting high-growth markets for rapid market share gains. These steps can be planned for in advance within the strategic framework we talked about earlier.

However, most small businesses don't plan for hypergrowth. It takes them by surprise. An example would be a small business that gets a shout-out from a social media influencer—and suddenly has a line out the door. What if that same business gets the attention of a major retailer, and suddenly Walmart or Costco wants to stock their goods? They may be blindsided and scramble to marshal the resources needed to scale up production so they can take advantage of that kind of partnership. Even if they manage to obtain the resources they need, they may run out of energy. Remember our discussion about energy and velocity at the end of the first chapter? You need *four times the energy* to simply *double* your velocity. That isn't always possible.

I saw a small Nashville-based publishing company in the 1980s stretched to the limit as a result of hypergrowth. They specialized in coffee table and regional-interest books, focusing on Tennessee history, sights, and culture—the kinds of books that might be interesting to locals or tourists but wouldn't have mass-market reach. Then, they happened to have one big hit.

In 1991, they published *Life's Little Instruction Book,* by H. Jackson Brown. Brown wrote it as a going-away gift to his son Adam when Adam went to college. That book was reviewed by the *New York Times* and became a bestseller. It sold more than ten million copies and was translated into more than thirty-three languages. Suddenly, this little local publisher was facing rapid growth. They went from having a little line of credit at the branch bank where I was working at the time to having a multimillion-dollar credit facility with participating banks to accommodate it all.

That level of growth proved unwieldy. They ended up selling to a larger publishing house and became an imprint under that bigger media umbrella. Now, they were still an operating company at that time—but they may have lacked the resources or energy to continue operating independently. From an operational standpoint, they simply couldn't accommodate the skyrocketing success.

It's very hard to sustain a business when you have a spike like that. If your service or product is validated by a major distribution channel, there's so much rapid change going on—with your customer base, your financing, your employees, and beyond. When you scale up that quickly, you get preoccupied with maintaining the operational side of things. For example, say Walmart wants to sell your products; that's exciting at first, but then you may start wondering, *How am I ever going to make enough product to deliver to one thousand stores?* That's when business owners tend to lose strategic direction.

On the other hand, if you're aware of your resources and marshaling them carefully, you can grow while controlling your speed. I've seen a wonderful example of this in my own community. When my family first moved here in the mid-1990s, the homes didn't have Hardie Plank–style siding. The siding was usually this composite wood material that wasn't as durable and was more prone to chipping and peeling paint, and even rot.

There was a gentleman in the area, Charlie Irwin, who would go around the neighborhood looking for homes with rotten boards. He'd knock on your door and say, "I'm the guy that does home painting and siding repair on this street, and it looks like you could use some help." By that time, the homeowner might have gotten a notice from the architectural control committee or whatever organization was responsible for upholding the neighborhood's appearance, telling them they had to fix their siding. Charlie was in the right spot at the right time, ready to meet the need. It was a flawless business model. He probably had a 90 percent market share in our neighborhood.

That was it—that was his entire business at the beginning. But then he started to grow. He had a son who joined the company and supported his growth. Today, they're a huge corporate company. It's not "Charlie Irwin Painting" but "CIP," and they do large-scale industrial painting projects well beyond my neighborhood; they're operating across the entire southeastern US.

When you look at where Charlie started, going door to door, that growth is pretty unbelievable. But when you break it down, it's logical. This is a business owner who strategically asked himself, "Where is the current opportunity? Okay, now what's the next opportunity? What equipment do I need? What people do I need? What resources do I need to expand?" He made his business decisions accordingly. As a result, the business grew but never exceeded its resource capacity.

Controlling your speed requires marshaling your resources like Charlie Irwin did. Those resources could include the following:

- **Energy.** Your own personal energy plays a big part. How much energy can you provide? How much energy do you need from others—can you do it on your own, or do you need a multiperson team? Especially in cases of failures stemming from hypergrowth, I think the gut reaction is to blame finances and say, "They ran out of money," but I think it's often a case of "They ran out of energy." This brings us back to chapter 1, "Energy."

- **People.** This plays into the energy question. If you don't have the energy to sustain independently, is it time to bring in others? How many? Do you need a lot of people behind you, or can you make do with fractional workers? When you get those people, how do you energize them? How do you motivate, inspire, and empower them? This is something I'll discuss in chapter 4, "Mass."

- **Suppliers.** What happens if Costco or Walmart wants to sell your products? You want to make sure you have suppliers that can keep up. Even when your business is small, reliable suppliers are critical to maintaining customer satisfaction. Unified orders can help streamline supply. At the same time, it's important to plan for supply chain disruptions. Global events like the COVID-19 pandemic, the worst supply chain disruption since the Second World War, can't be foreseen but they can be planned for. What do you do if supply chain issues strike? How do you keep your customers happy? I'll discuss this in chapter 3, "Force."

- **Organizational capacity.** Even if you have the energy, people, and capital, they won't do you any good if they are not properly allocated and funneled. When organizations move too fast, they tend to become unmanageable. You've got to make sure your workflows are streamlined; you've got to keep an eye on that balance sheet; you've got to manage your profits and losses. Plus, you need the right people taking the right actions at the right times to keep it all clicking along. You need organizational cohesion—something we'll talk about more in chapter 5, "Inertia."

- **Capital.** This is a more obvious one that most people jump to first. Do you have the right level of capital? Many businesses want to get there very quickly, and that typically involves a capital raise. Eager entrepreneurs give pitches to secure angel investors, get a ton of money, and build a big team. That's not bad, necessarily. It lets you cover more ground a lot faster than someone working out of their garage alone. But even businesses that have raised enormous sums can lose it all if they aren't marshaling their financial resources effectively. Financial planning is a big part of the process, and I'll cover some of the hurdles business owners face on the financial side of things in chapter 8, "Leverage."

Creating a Plan to Control Your Velocity's Direction, Magnitude, and Speed

Strategizing the direction and speed of your velocity in a deliberate way can save you a lot of headaches as a business owner. Once you've got those strategic elements in place, it will be easier to see which business decisions are smart and serve your purposes—and which ones can get in the way of your big picture goals. Where to begin? I suggest a business plan.

A business plan is a written document that outlines your business's objectives and describes how you plan to achieve them. It's like a road map for your business, covering your USP, your target customer, and more. Your business plan helps you move in a defined direction deliberately. It doesn't just point your business in that direction; it also outlines the resources you need to go in that direction, like capital or people.

Traditional business plans cover three-, five-, or ten-year periods. I usually recommend small business owners create a three-year plan, which seems like a realistic forward-looking time frame. Having that set period in mind—knowing by when you want to achieve what—helps to control your business growth in a deliberate way. This can help prevent hypergrowth and all its pitfalls.

Now, as you develop your business plan, you also want to take into account external forces that might impact your business. This can include elements like the economic climate or market competition. I'll talk about those forces in more detail in the next chapter.

I recommend supplementing a business plan with a SWOT (strengths, weaknesses, opportunities, and threats) analysis. This is a framework you can use to evaluate your business's competitive position and to support strategic planning. A comprehensive SWOT analysis addresses internal and external factors, current and future. Like your business plan, it can also help you avoid bad decisions—for example, decisions that are rapid response, instead of direction-aware.

Many businesses fall into this "rapid response" trap. They have a sense of FOMO (fear of missing out) and worry that the next big thing is going to pass them by, so they jump on fads or trends and make unwise business decisions.

For example, when Apple launched the iPod, a lot of other companies jumped on the bandwagon and brought out similar products in a reactive response. One example is Dell, which brought out the Dell DJ. I was a little bit stingy about investing in an Apple iPod and got a Dell DJ. Unfortunately, from a SWOT standpoint,

Dell was not equipped to enter the digital music space in the same way that Apple was. As a result, the Dell DJ died a very quick death because it was not a competitive product. I still have mine, though, and my family teases me about it to this day.

🧪 TO THE LAB!

Check out the "In Your Lab" resource section at the conclusion of chapter 2, and you'll find links to both a Business Plan Template and SWOT Analysis Template.

Having your business plan and SWOT analysis in hand will help keep you going in the right direction, at the right pace. You can always come back to your written strategy when making hard business decisions, ensuring that you know where you want to be going and that the choices you're making are the right ones to help you get there.

But beware: the business planning process isn't a onetime thing. It requires ongoing evaluation of where your business is currently and where it's going in the future—especially taking into account the various forces around your business that can impact it, which I'll discuss in the next chapter. You need to revisit your business plan regularly. Just because you think you've got the "perfect" plan now doesn't mean it's going to be perfect one year from now.

This was a standing joke at one bank I worked for. Every fall, we'd have our strategic planning session, where the leaders would sit down together to work out everything from each team's annual commitments to their budgets. It would take multiple iterations until that strategic plan was finalized. At the end, the gentleman in charge—a very Southern man—would always say, "Well, what we have here is the perfect plan."

At that point, we'd all chuckle to ourselves—because we knew there was no such thing. In that moment, it might have felt perfect. We wanted to think it was. After all, we had just put in all this work to formulate the plan. Everybody was energized. We were all focused on the plan and what we had to do to carry it out, and each individual had a perfect sense of where they were headed. But we hadn't *engaged* with the plan yet. We hadn't yet experienced—or even anticipated—all the forces that might impact that plan, from bank failures to global pandemics.

Business planning is a dynamic process. That doesn't mean it's fruitless. It can keep you on track and, just as importantly, it can instill confidence. Especially for a solopreneur or small business owner, having a plan can be really reassuring. You can tell yourself, "I've got the perfect plan," even as you smile to yourself because you know: anything can happen. It's going to get messed up. But still, I think you have to believe in that perfect plan to get that confidence, especially when you're starting out.

Velocity Can Be Impacted by Many Different Forces

By regularly revisiting your plan, you'll gain awareness of what's going on in your business and encourage yourself to make decisions that align with your goals. This is especially important as your business picks up. Our perception of things changes dramatically when we're moving quickly. Consider this concept from the Albert Einstein–level perspective and think about how objects flatten or time slows down at high speeds.

When you're a business owner in the midst of everyday operations, your perception of what is and isn't important may shift. What you're paying attention to as you're moving may not be a clear picture or the reality you're dealing with—you're moving so fast that things aren't as they appear to be. Factors impacting your business present differently than what they really are. That's how you might end up like Dell, getting caught up in the whirlwind trend of digital music and putting out the Dell DJ—not realizing that your product can't compete with the Apple iPod.

If you have the energy needed to pursue entrepreneurship, you don't want to burn that energy up like a pinwheel firework, flaming in circles. Be very purposeful about your goals: how far you want to get and how quickly you want to get there. Draft your business plan; write your SWOT analysis; deliberately marshal your resources. This is how you'll *consciously* move your business in a given direction at a determined pace. This is how you'll control your velocity.

Now, there are many external factors that will impact your velocity as you go. Remember, velocity is a vector measurement, addressing both size and direction. If we look at velocity as an arrow, the length represents the distance, the way it points signifies its direction, and speed is usually depicted by an axis reflecting a time horizon. All kinds of forces can influence the arrow's length and the way it's pointing. Some of those forces can be anticipated, while others are impossible for even the savviest business owner to see coming. The COVID-19 pandemic is one example. But, reassuringly, most vectors *are* foreseeable—and business planning can help you prepare for them. Let's talk about those forces in chapter 3.

🧪 IN YOUR LAB

At the start of this chapter, I asked you: How fast are you going and where? The Bizzics website has some resources to help you determine your business's velocity—the direction your business is pointed in and how fast it's going to get there:

- **Business Plan Template:** Create a road map for your business's future.

- **Strengths, Weaknesses, Opportunities, and Threats (SWOT) Analysis:** Assess your business's competitive edge.

THE BIZZICS WAY

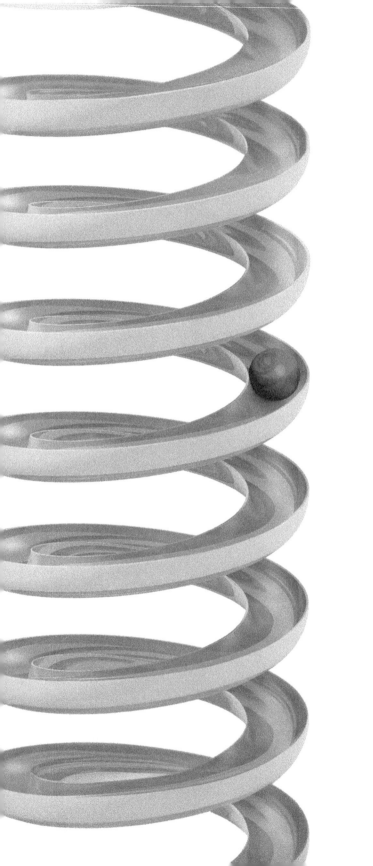

Force

I f business ownership were easy, everybody would be doing it. The reality is that, despite your greatest vision and most detailed planning to achieve that vision, the business landscape contains all kinds of forces that work counter to your vision. Don't get me wrong: there are also forces that surprisingly propel your vision in ways you could never have anticipated—but even those have their own challenges. Even with a strong plan and confidence, as an entrepreneur you enter an uncertain world of unseen forces that must be managed.

A look at force from the physics side of things can help explain what I mean. Let's start with Newton's first law of motion. This states that an object will stay stationary or on the path it's on until some unequal force moves it in another direction. Newton's first law of motion is also known as the law of inertia—a topic I'll discuss more in chapter 5.

For now, I want to focus on this core concept: when force is enacted on a moving object with mass, that object's velocity changes.

Like velocity, force is a vector quantity. It has not only a magnitude but also a direction.

Physics also has something called "net force." This is the sum of all the velocities—all the different vectors—acting on an object. Forces in the world can come from a multitude of directions, and when those forces impact your business, they can also send it in all kinds of crazy directions, some desirable and some undesirable.

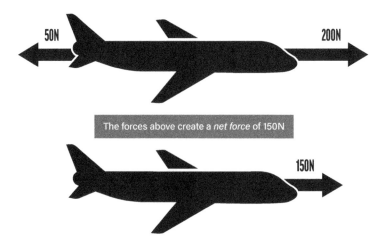

The forces above create a *net force* of 150N

Have you ever been on a commercial flight and the pilot comes on the loudspeaker and says, "Ladies and gentlemen, we've got some turbulence ahead, but we're going to take the aircraft around it"—and, as a result of that detour, you land five minutes later than scheduled? Alternatively, have you ever had a flight land twenty minutes early, thanks to some helpful tailwinds?

Airline pilots deal with competing forces every time they take an aircraft up. They must be vigilant for the unexpected gust or air pocket that could affect passenger safety and arrival times. My most frustrating flight experience was the time our aircraft could not land in Denver because of a hailstorm. We were rerouted to Albuquerque, and I missed one of my dream concerts—Steely Dan at Red Rocks. I was safe, though, which was the more important thing.

Your job as a business owner is to manage those counterforces to the best of your ability, so you can land that plane safely. You're the pilot. New business owners need to understand that they're entering a dynamic environment that's always changing. When some vector impacts your business, it can impact your business trajectory. The direction your business is headed in has changed, and it will continue in that direction (desirable or undesirable) until *you* enact some force of your own to counter it—and control that net force.

Now, as I mentioned, there are forces you can't anticipate, like COVID-19. Due to the pandemic, businesses of all kinds, all over the world, faced unexpected shutdowns, supply chain disruptions, and shifts in consumer demand. Other businesses capitalized on this momentous vector. Sales of athleisure took off. Zoom became everybody's go-to mode of communication. Delivery services skyrocketed.

But COVID-19 is just one force. There are many other vectors that are constantly going to be influencing your business and impacting its velocity—its direction, magnitude, and speed. You want to make sure you're not blindsided by these forces. That means recognizing that your business operates in a dynamic context and adjusting your original plan constantly.

Anticipating the types of vectors that will inevitably impact your business, especially as you're getting it started, can help. These are things you want to think about even as you draft your business plan. Let's look at what those might be.

> ## 🔎 KEY BUSINESS QUESTION:
>
> How do you stay aware of the surrounding business environment and calibrate accordingly?

Anticipating the Many Forces That Will Impact Your Business

Starting a business can feel chaotic at times, especially when you begin to consider all the external forces that may inevitably influence your business trajectory. Here's the thing: you aren't at the mercy of these external vectors. Yes, they're going to have an impact on your business. But you can respond with a force of your own.

Take the COVID-19 example. Many restaurants shuttered during the pandemic, notably in major cities like New York and Los Angeles. This could have spelled doom for many (and did for some). However, savvy restaurant owners reacted to the force of this vector with their own opposing force—they shifted their business models, turning to delivery and curbside pickup to stay afloat.

If you encounter a vector like COVID-19 and you don't *do* something about it, if you fail to react with your own counterforce, you lose control of the direction your business is headed. You lose control of your net velocity. A restaurateur that didn't shift to takeout or delivery during the pandemic probably didn't make it.

I look at it like an old pinball machine—I mean the *really* old pinball machines, with a physical metal ball inside, and all these little switches to pull to flick levers inside the machine. If the metal ball came whizzing down the machine and it came close to one of those levers, you could flick a switch to control the right lever and it would kick up, whack the metal ball (if you timed it right—which wasn't always easy), and send the ball whizzing back in another direction.

So, you'd have that little metal ball banging around inside the machine, running into obstacles, bouncing off levers as you switched them, and—hopefully—staying on the board and not falling into the pit at the bottom. As the player, you had a big part in controlling the ball's trajectory. The key was to enact the right force on the ball, using the right lever, at the right time. When the ball crashed into something and came hurtling down the machine in one direction, you had to engage a lever to enact an opposing force and send that ball back up in another direction.

I still remember what a rush it was to control the trajectory of that little metal ball and get it *just right*. When you hit a jackpot, the whole machine would go crazy—lights would blink on and off, bells would chime, and you'd see your player name in big letters on the high-score board. If you let the ball drop, because you neglected your levers—you didn't enact the right counterforces in time—you lost. If you were lucky, it was only your first ball; back then, a dollar bought you three balls, so you got to play three rounds. But if it was your last ball, your stomach would drop, because you knew you were out of chances.

You had to pay attention to the forces in the game that were controlling that little metal ball's trajectory—or you'd lose. I even saw people lift up the entire machine to try to save a ball in a last-minute panic. The same is true in business: you have to pay attention to all the forces that can impact your business's trajectory—or you'll lose. You don't want to be stuck trying to lift up the entire pinball machine to keep that from happening.

Not paying attention to these vectors can be a business's downfall. I don't want to sound dramatic, but it's true. Say there's a major change in the economic environment, like a recession. This will influence consumer purchasing power. People spend less. As a result, your business will earn less, and your cash flow will slow down. This can lead to a cycle of taking on loans or lines of credits to maintain cash flow to keep up with operational costs like production and wages. In the worst-case scenario, business owners get behind with this kind of borrowing and just never get caught up. I've seen it happen before, and it's a painful moment.

On the brighter side, being aware of these vectors and responding to them appropriately—by flicking the lever on that pinball machine—can help you pave the path to greater success. Take something like an emerging trend in the competitive market. If you track that trend and find a way to integrate it into your business that makes sense, you might be able to increase your market share.

That doesn't mean you have to hop on every trend. Remember the cautionary tale of the Dell DJ? That's the kind of reactive business decision that comes from trend-following. However, it's important to be *aware* of the trends so that when one comes that *does* make sense for your business, you don't lose a competitive edge or miss out on market share.

Knowledge of external vectors helps you better control your own counterforces in responding to them. For now, I want to focus on some of the vectors that will present themselves early in your business development. At the end of this chapter, I'll give you some pointers on how to research, anticipate, and prepare for these shifting vectors.

ECONOMIC ENVIRONMENT

The economic environment your business operates in is going to shift and can impact your success in a big way. The economic environment is very much like the physics concept of pulsating worlds. Systems are constantly expanding and contracting, often in a certain rhythm. This may be nearly imperceptible to humans, because of the magnitude of the systems involved and the fact that the expansion and contraction at work may be small relative to the system's total mass. However, sometimes the expansion or contraction is apparent.

Demand for products and services changes over time. Businesses respond with supply that often outpaces demand, sometimes because they just get too optimistic. This is considered an expansion, until business owners realize that they have overshot the market. Economic growth takes a break, while supply and demand rebalance (contraction). It is a pulsating, often rhythmic, phenomenon.

A shifting economic environment can present both hurdles and opportunities. Let's take the example of low interest rates. Yes, even money is subject to supply and demand forces, and oversupply as well. For small businesses, a time of low interest rates can be a wonderful opportunity for growth and expansion. They can take advantage of lower borrowing costs to pay off debts or take out a new loan at a lower rate, for example. They might use that loan to buy new property, production equipment, or inventory—whatever they need to expand. On the other hand, rising interest rates can cause problems. Higher interest means it can take longer to pay back business loans.

The idea of the economic environment is so broad that it affects nearly every aspect of your business, not just interest rates. It affects how much people are buying from you and what you are paying for labor, raw materials, and services that support your business.

REGULATORY ISSUES

Regulatory issues impact pretty much every industry in one way or another. Some industries, like finance or pharmaceuticals, face more red tape than others. But even if you're just opening a neighborhood restaurant, you've got regulatory issues to contend with. You've got to pass the health and safety inspection, for example. If you want to serve alcohol, you've got to get a liquor license. You've also got to make sure you're in line with fire code and labor law. These legislative issues stack up quickly.

I've seen regulatory changes destabilize an entire industry right here in Nashville. When I was working in downtown Nashville, my offices were about two blocks from Lower Broadway, a center of activity in town. It was also the starting point for the beer bikes—multipassenger taverns on wheels that people pedal while they drink—and party barges, passenger platforms on the backs of heavy-duty trucks.

I'd be sitting in my office, and around ten o'clock every morning, I'd hear the beer bikes and party barges fire up. There was music, alcohol, and a *lot* of excited partygoers (including quite a few bachelor and bachelorette parties on any given day).

When you put together a lot of people plus alcohol—on moving vehicles, no less—things tend to get a little out of control. In response to the growing risks, the city slowed down the issuance of party vehicle licenses and, in some cases, even rescinded them. What looked like a fail-proof business model just a few years back is now more questionable. It's not the sure shot it was, as the regulatory environment continues to shift.

TAXATION

Taxation is technically part of the regulatory equation, but it's such a significant point, I think it deserves its own spot on the list. Understanding and living within tax laws to minimize tax liability is a way of life for small business owners. This helps with business capitalization. Growth funding will either come from money retained in the business or from borrowing; most people would prefer to have their own money to fund their growth. It's not about trying to "cheat" the government. It's simply about trying to address that, after you've paid your business expenses, there's a pile of money there, and 20 to 25 percent of that goes to Uncle Sam—which means less capital stays in your business. Smart tax planning helps to retain that money, reducing the risk that you'll have to borrow to grow.

Taxes are something you've got to grapple with from the very start, when you're figuring out what *kind* of business you're setting up. The way you're taxed as a limited liability company (LLC) is different from the way you're taxed as a corporation, for example. Your tax residence also makes a difference. *Where* your business is incorporated impacts how much tax you'll have to pay. Certain states are known for having friendlier tax environments for entrepreneurs than others.

The size of your business can also impact what type of structure is right for you. You might start as an LLC and later restructure once you're bigger, for instance. While it's usually best to consult a tax professional for personally tailored advice, you can also learn about tax changes through small business associations—I mention a couple of options at the end of this chapter in the section "Tips for Tracking Vectors."

From the outset, you can choose the appropriate entity structure for you: C corp, S corp, partnership, LLC, sole proprietorship. Each will have its distinct taxation features, which you should understand. Stay educated about specific tax *policies too*. Many policies present a counterforce to your business objectives. However, there are just as many, if not more, designed to serve as tailwinds (support) for your business objectives—things like accelerated depreciation, hiring incentives, and local tax credits for investment.

I recommend meeting with your certified public accountant (CPA) or tax advisor annually, before the start of the next fiscal year. It is a time for strategy and planning, so you can ensure you are taking advantage of all the options available to you. At the same time, be careful about building your business around tax policies, because policies change with the political climate. If they're sudden, such changes can be devastating to your business.

COMPETITIVE MARKET

The competitive environment is always changing, with new entrants to the market arriving and different ways of doing business taking hold. The used car market is one example. You used to go to a lot, see some cars, pick one, and go. The industry has evolved thanks to specialized competitors that provide not only a car but also the kinds of extras that were once expected only with a new vehicle—like a warranty. CarMax is a great example. All the company's used cars are CarMax Certified and come with a four-thousand-mile or ninety-day warranty.[15] This protection for a used vehicle was unheard of back when I was buying my first car.

The fundamental lesson is that every industry has a constant drive to create stronger value propositions for customers. No matter how good you think you may be, I promise you that the world as you know it is changing thanks to ambitious innovators.

There are many market research tools that can help you keep track of an industry's competitive dynamics, emerging trends, and potential risks. I've seen banks use these when underwriting loans. I personally like Vertical IQ, which I talk about more later in the chapter. Trade publications are another way to learn about the competitive market. Trade associations are close to the action and get firsthand insights into industry changes from their members, who are on the front lines.

🧪 TO THE LAB!

I've included some additional resources to help you understand competitiveness in the "In Your Lab" resource section at the conclusion of chapter 3. See the Competitive Advantage Plan and Competitor Analysis Template.

---

15   CarMax, "Love Your Car Guarantee," n.d., accessed September 25, 2023, https://www.carmax.com/faq/warranties.

SUPPLIERS

Whatever your business type, odds are you'll need to work with suppliers of some kind. If you're running a restaurant, you're going to have people bringing in your meat, produce, and bakery goods. If you're running a clothing store, you've got to source apparel from somewhere. If you're a contractor, you've got to rely on supplies of raw goods like timber. Without these goods, you can't run your business. You want to make sure that your suppliers consistently provide products that meet your quality standards. Investigate what quality control measures are in place and what oversight, if any, you have over those measures.

You can't take supply for granted. For one thing, suppliers themselves may be unreliable. If you find that a vendor is repeatedly late or not giving you the goods you need, you'll have to shift. It's also important to consider a supplier's financial health—if they're operating under unsound economic conditions, there's a risk of operations (and your supply) being impacted.

On top of that, there are larger forces that can cause supply chain issues that are beyond your and the supplier's control. Again, the COVID-19 pandemic is a good example here. National lockdowns often slowed or completely stopped the flow of raw materials, disrupting manufacturing and interrupting supply chains. Conflicts like the war in Ukraine are another example. The country's role as the breadbasket to the world was dangerously interrupted in 2022, raising the risk of food supply disruption in other parts of the world.

EMPLOYEES

Employees are another vector that some business owners may take for granted. The worker shortages following the COVID-19 pandemic are a testament to the fact that you can't assume you'll have ready and willing workers available to keep your business moving. There are also economic factors that impact the availability of employees. Wages are a prime example. Broadly speaking, an increase in employee wages can be good, improving consumers' purchasing power and boosting consumer spending. However, businesses must then deal with higher overhead costs.

Then, there are unemployment rates. When unemployment is low, businesses may struggle to find people—and will likely have to pay more for top talent. On the other side of the equation, high unemployment usually makes it easier to find workers—but it also is linked to less favorable economic trends like slower consumer spending, since unemployment negatively impacts households' disposable income and reduces purchasing power. As you can see, many of these vectors become intertwined—for instance, the economic environment can impact everything from your employees to your customers.

Finally, remember that employees are unique. There are going to be generational differences between what boomers versus Gen X versus millennials versus Gen Z want to be satisfied and engaged at work. Value propositions in the workplace have shifted postpandemic, with many employees, especially younger generations, wanting a more "human deal" at work, like deeper connections and greater flexibility.[16] Are you able to offer the right environment for the workforce that will serve your clients best?

---

16   Swetha Venkataramani, "Make Way for a More Human-Centric Employee Value Proposition," Gartner, May 13, 2021, https://www.gartner.com/smarterwithgartner/make-way-for-a-more-human-centric-employee-value-proposition.

CUSTOMER MINDSET

Customer mindsets shift over time, for various reasons. By understanding the evolving customer mindset, you can make sure your business keeps up with their wants and needs. Take a showdown like Netflix versus Blockbuster. When Netflix came onto the scene, they saw a customer desire to simplify video rentals; people craved greater convenience. Netflix delivered—literally—by sending DVDs straight to consumers' mailboxes. No more trips to the Blockbuster video store were needed. Then, technological advances spurred the change further, as improvements in internet speed and accessibility made streaming possible. Netflix no longer had to send a DVD to someone's home address (an era that younger users never even experienced). With streaming, consumers could access movies and TV shows on their home devices.

One example of shifting consumer mindsets I observed dates to the midnineties, when the dot-com era was exploding. At the same time, athletic wear was booming. Since the release of Air Jordans, sneaker culture and athletic wear had become big business. There was a gentleman in Tennessee who wanted to take advantage of that trend and started an athletic-wear company. They sold sports footwear and apparel, but their specialty was team logo items. Their shops stocked gear with logos of all the area sports teams, from Tennessee State to Vanderbilt University. If you wanted team apparel, this was your go-to shop.

The business started with one shop in Nashville and expanded quickly to about eight locations. However, the retail landscape was changing, as e-commerce was entering the picture. For whatever reason, this sport shop never started an online store. They kept putting it off and got stuck; their business took a hit, and they had to scale back as a result. Last I checked, there were only four store locations still operating. Now, if this store had been more intentional with examining customer preferences, they might have hopped on the e-commerce bandwagon and sustained greater growth.

SOCIOCULTURAL CONTEXT

Changes in consumer mindsets and sociocultural shifts go hand in hand. The move toward work-from-home is one of the most obvious examples. The COVID-19 pandemic accelerated this shift significantly. I think this shift also influenced the more casual workplace culture we see today. People from home certainly aren't wearing suits to sit at their laptops, and some of that attitude has trickled into offices too.

When looking at broader social and cultural contexts—or any of these "big picture" vectors—it's always important to consider the impact on your business, both immediately and in the future. A shift that may not influence your business in two years could influence it in ten years. Again, the case of Blockbuster and Netflix is a good example here. It's not like Netflix appeared and put Blockbuster out of business overnight. But, with time, that's pretty much what happened. So, you have to consider: What's the magnitude of the vector that's going to weigh on you? Is the influence overnight, or is it a longer process?

TECHNOLOGICAL IMPACT

Finally, there's the technological vector—one that is getting a lot of attention these days as people discuss artificial intelligence and how it's going to influence various industries, from marketing to healthcare. Nashville, where I live, is a big music town, and the changing technologies used to make music have altered the landscape here drastically. The music industry today doesn't look anything like it did twenty years ago. It used to be that a musician would spend days in an expensive recording studio trying to get one sound just right. Now, the technology needed to create music is simpler and more accessible. You've got kids making music out of their bedrooms and going viral on social media with one song.

The technology piece is going to get more and more drastic as we move ahead. The rate of technological advancement is increasing, and the ways we can use different technologies seem to be proliferating. Tech is also getting more accessible. So small business owners can't assume that some fancy new technology like ChatGPT will be available only to huge corporations with big tech budgets. These tools are available for smaller businesses too. You don't want to let the opportunities they may unlock pass you by.

Tips for Tracking Vectors

If you look at all the vectors that impact your business, there's a lot to account for. Think of the graph we used to demonstrate velocity in chapter 2. Now, let's add all these external forces to it. It might look something like this:

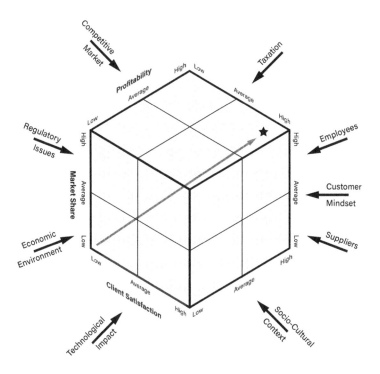

How do you plan to track all these vectors and stay on top of them throughout the entirety of your business journey? It might seem like a big job on top of the big job you're already doing of starting and managing a business. But it's a must. The good news: There are some excellent resources to help you track all those external vectors. Here are some ideas to get you started:

- **Read, read, read:** Stay on top of current events. This can help you track big picture vectors, like the economic environment. Read the business and financial news, but also keep an eye on the broader news. Issues like pandemics or wars will trickle down to impact vectors that influence your day-to-day, from supply chains to employee availability and consumer purchasing power.

- **Join industry trade organizations:** Industry organizations are a great way to learn about regulatory changes that impact your business and to keep up with emerging trends that impact competitive dynamics. This could mean joining multiple organizations. For example, if you're a contractor, you might join the Associated Builders & Contractors (ABC), Associated General Contractors of America (AGC), and American Institute of Constructors (AIC)—and those are only a few of the many options available.

- **Participate in small business networks:** While industry organizations can give you industry-specific information, small business organizations can give you broader updates about issues that impact entrepreneurs of all kinds—like changes in tax laws. Look up your local SBA or US Chamber of Commerce branch for a good starting point.

- **Take advantage of market research tools:** One tool I like is Vertical IQ, which provides profiles of all kinds of industries. You can approach Vertical IQ and get a full industry report of all the competitive forces, emerging trends, and risk factors in your industry. It's about a twenty-five- to thirty-page report, and much more cost efficient than other marketing research firms.

- **Know when to ask for help:** Before you make any big shifts in your business, if you're feeling uncertain—talk to a professional. Tax structures are a great example. If you don't know what kind of business structure to set up and are confused about the tax implications of the various structures, your best bet is usually to consult a tax attorney. Investing a little bit now can save you trouble later.

> ## ⚗ TO THE LAB!
>
> I've included some additional resources to help you track vectors in the "In Your Lab" resource section at the conclusion of chapter 3. You'll find a Multi-Vector Analysis, Ripple Effects Template, and Resilience Planner.

Building Mass to Help Manage External Forces

In chapter 2, we looked at velocity, your business's primary vector. It determines where your business is going and how fast it's growing. Now, we've talked about all the other vectors that can throw your business off course. From shifts in the economic environment to regulatory changes, these vectors are inevitably going to impact you in some way, small or large. While you can't predict and prepare for every vector—COVID-19 being one example—there *are* many that you can anticipate.

When you sense a shift due to one of those vectors, it's up to you to course correct that little metal ball in your pinball machine. Ideally, you'll be able to find a way that doesn't involve lifting up the entire machine! You can start by educating yourself about the ever-changing forces that can impact your business using the tips above, plus the tools in the "In Your Lab" section at the end of this chapter.

Another thing that can help? Creating sufficient mass in your business. Mass is what will help your business stay the course when outside forces are enacted on it. It's also a critical part of the equation (literally!) for building momentum for your business. We've already talked about velocity; the last couple of chapters have been all about speed, direction, and countervailing forces. Next, we're going to talk about mass. Remember, the formula: momentum = mass x velocity.

Mass is going to bring us to our holy grail, what every business owner seeks: momentum. Let's talk about the how you can build the mass to get there next.

🝆 IN YOUR LAB

At the start of this chapter, I asked how you remain aware of your business environment, so you can calibrate accordingly. I've given you some tips on how to monitor the vectors that impact your business above. The Bizzics website has some additional resources to help you maintain oversight of those vectors:

- **Competitive Advantage Plan:** Define what makes your business stand out from the crowd.

- **Competitor Analysis Template:** Determine how you stack up compared to others in your market.

- **Multi-Vector Analysis:** Determine the vectors that are impacting your business.

- **Ripple Effects Template:** Find out what ripple effects are impacting your business.

- **Resilience Planner:** Can your business hold up in the face of outside forces? Let's find out how resilient you are.

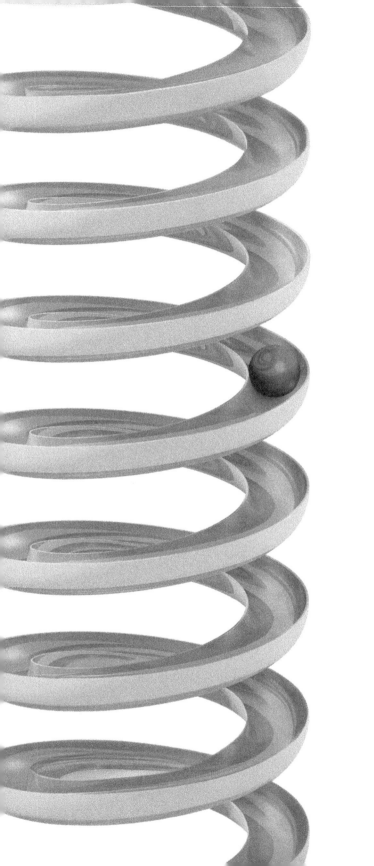

CHAPTER 4

Mass

A consistent feature of the great mythological quests is that the seeker of truth or treasure confronts a riddle or paradox that must be resolved before they can continue on their journey, dodging the dragon or crossing the deadly abyss. I don't know anyone who didn't laugh hysterically at the random questions of the oracle in *Monty Python and the Holy Grail*. So, my riddle for you, the earnest seeker of momentum in your business, is this: How can a small business be massive? The scientific definition of mass is a critical part of the answer, and provides the insight we need to dig deeper.

Mass is a fundamental property of all matter. In effect, mass is the resistance that a body of matter offers upon the application of a force. The more mass an object has, the smaller the change of its speed, position, or direction when a force is applied to it.

In my conversations with Marcus, mass proved to be one of the trickier topics. Marcus challenged me, asking "What does mass even look like in a business context? What does it mean?" One thing I'm sure of: In business, mass isn't a question of *size*. After all, a volleyball and a bowling ball are about the same size. Yet, one has much greater weight and density. A small business can have just as much mass as a major corporation. Size isn't the answer.

It's about what's on the *inside*. A bowling ball is not hollow. It's tightly packed with various dense materials. In contrast, a volleyball is only filled with air—and while air also has mass to it, it lacks the density of the materials inside of a bowling ball.

In the business world, achieving mass requires mimicking that dense, tightly packed core. How are you going to achieve that kind of mass in your company? It starts with you. Just as we discussed in chapter 1, where you are both the source and distributor of entrepreneurial energy in your business, the mass of your business begins with you.

Inevitably, you will hit a point in your business where you realize you can't go it alone. This is an opportunity to build mass. But hold on! I don't mean that you should just hire anybody and everybody to build mass. It's not quite that simple. How *do* you build mass with the proper density? You already know what I'm going to say: let's look to physics for the answer.

Mass has two key components: the density of the elements and the strength of the bonds among the molecules. There's superlight matter like helium. Then, you've got elements like osmium, the densest element on the periodic table. To give you an idea, this metal is about twice as dense as lead and heavier than gold.[17]

---

17   Anne Helmenstine, "What Is the Heaviest or Densest Element on the Periodic Table?," *Science Notes*, August 26, 2021, https://sciencenotes.org/what-is-the-heaviest-or-densest-element-on-the-periodic-table/.

You have to be really aware of the materials you are packing in your proverbial bowling ball. What matter are you putting inside to achieve the density and weight desired?

When you're building mass, you want those high-quality, heavy-weight materials in your business—employees with the fitting vision, values, and skills. It's then on you to nurture the bonds within the organization and to continually invest in employees so they continue to add mass to your organization. However, before you can do any of that, you've got to start with yourself.

> ⌕ **KEY BUSINESS QUESTION:**
>
> How can you ensure that your business is massive enough to easily roll through obstacles, instead of getting derailed?

Building Your Team: Your Nucleus of Protons and Neutrons

All matter is made of atoms, and every atom has a dense inner core, the nucleus, which is filled with protons and neutrons. The nucleus accounts for about 99.9 percent of the atom's mass. The rest of the atom is just a kind of electron fog.

If you think of your business as an atom, the nucleus is where you want to focus when you start building mass. It starts with you, the business owner—you are part of that nucleus, along with the energy you bring, your experience and leadership ability, and the values you articulate. Your vision has a certain density to it as well, seen in the strength of your value proposition and the sheer number of people you intend to help with your unique offering. An atom's protons are stable and do not break down or decay on their own. So, we might consider you the protons in the nucleus. After all, it's your business; you aren't going anywhere.

The neutrons, on the other hand, are not stable in the same way. Adding neutrons—in this case, more people—can increase the atom's mass. However, you also have to consider the density question. There's no point bringing in more people just for the sake of it. You've got to make sure you're bringing in the *right* people at the right time, and that they align with your cause.

Finding the right people starts with having the right vision—one that others can coalesce around. That's how you'll attract people who share the values that make up your business's core. You can then create a tightly packed mass of people around that core, people who are as buzzing with energy as you are about your business. It's your very own bowling ball—one you can chuck down the lane and knock any pins out of the way with.

It all starts with a vision. A testament to this fact is seen in the story of my friends David and Marlene Ssebulime, founders of Raise the Roof Academy in Uganda. In 2013, David asked me to deliver leadership training at the school in Bwassandeku, Uganda. David and Marlene founded the school in 2011, starting with thirty students and two teachers. By 2013, enrollment had grown to 300, with 150 of the students sponsored by American benefactors. David was determined to make effective leadership skills—for students and teachers alike— part of the academy's foundation. What happened over the next ten years is truly remarkable.

First, let me give you a little background because it goes to the heart of the bonding power of a thoughtful mission and vision— and demonstrates how bringing people together around well-defined values can start to build mass.

David was born in Kampala, Uganda. His father was a Christian pastor who drew the ire of Idi Amin for seeking justice for women who had been raped by Amin's army. His father was ultimately imprisoned and tortured by Amin. After Amin lost power in 1978, David's father was released and resumed his ministry, often in remote parts of Uganda.

Flash forward to 1984. After preaching Christmas eve services in Bwassandeku, a farming village outside Masaka—at the time Uganda's third largest city—David's father was run off the road and killed by Amin's successor, Apollo Obote. David's mother was left with eleven children to raise. Through a series of gracious and loving acts by others, David established a role as a drummer in the African Children's Choir, touring the world and, later, gaining the sponsorship of a loving couple who guided him to the US. There, he earned a college degree and a master of divinity from Vanderbilt University.

When David and Marlene founded Raise the Roof Academy in 2011, they established it in the same place where his father had been killed, extending his father's mission to improve the lives of impoverished Ugandans. Their motivation was filled with meaning, which they shared through their mission and vision:

- The mission of Raise the Roof Academy: *We advocate for children and community development one household at a time.*

- The vision of Raise the Roof Academy: *To see generations of empowered children lead community change and share their passion with the world.*

I'll talk about how David and Marlene empowered others in the next chapter. Here, I want to emphasize their mission and vision. The organization's values are meaningful, informed by an impactful story. There is a reason I harped so much on mission, vision, and values in the first chapter, and this is exactly why—those components you establish at the start of your business have a trickle-down effect that can influence your efforts, like your ability to build mass, later.

A weighty mission and vision are sure to create energy. Given the personal import of this endeavor for him, David can wake up buzzing every day. And that energy is magnetic. It draws in other people—the kind of people who are likely to contribute to an organization's mass.

Hiring a Team for Small Businesses

David has been able to attract others to his mission, even from halfway across the world. He's the reason I left Nashville and went to Uganda to teach leadership principles to local community leaders. And I'm not the only one David convinced. Thanks to his energy and clarity of vision, David has been able to get many others on board this initiative (which has led to great success—as you'll see when I continue his story in chapter 5).

However, that success didn't come solely from bringing people on board. It relied on *bonding* those people, uniting them around that mission and vision, in a cohesive way. By connecting people closely, David increased his organization's mass—and its density.

Mass and density are proportional, so if one increases, the other increases. Take a substance like carbon. Carbon comes in various forms, with various densities and masses.

Simply hiring isn't enough: consider how team members are bonded. You want them closely united in their pursuit of a shared vision and mission.

Those different forms have varying strengths. One form of carbon is graphite—like what you'd find in a pencil. The density of graphite is 2.3 g>cm³. Another form of carbon is diamond. The density of a diamond is significantly greater, at 3.5 g>cm³.

People always marvel about diamonds and how they're the hardest naturally occurring substance on earth (there's a good reason that engagement ring you bought cost such a pretty penny)! Diamonds don't gain that strength from the carbon they're made of alone— it comes from their carbon density, the super-tight way the carbon atoms inside of them are packed.

If you want that kind of strength in your organization, the strength of a diamond, you've got to consider the density—which correlates with your mass. Simply hiring people isn't enough. You want to consider how those people are bonded. You want them closely packed together, metaphorically speaking, united in their pursuit of a shared vision and mission. The superglue of this kind of bonding is shared values—and shared experiences in authentically living the mission.

START WITH THE RIGHT VALUES

If you want heavyweight individuals in your organization, the ones that really contribute to mass—adding not only size but also density, like osmium—you've got to bring on people who share your organization's values, the pillars that uphold your vision. Why do values matter? They bond people together. That's how you create the density associated with mass—through bonding. It's also important to remember that certain materials simply won't bond and will remain like oil and water. Values-based hiring can help avoid this issue.

Values-based hiring has become a big topic in recent years, as organizations have come to recognize the power that comes with coalescing workers around common values. Two companies that get it right? Chick-fil-A and Ben & Jerry's. These organizations are at opposite ends of the spectrum when it comes to the values they espouse. Chick-fil-A has strong religious foundations; the restaurants remain closed on Sundays, to give employees a day off to worship, if they so choose. Their core values focus on pillars like service, teamwork, and being purpose driven.[18]

The values espoused by Ben & Jerry's are another story. They focus on points like social and economic justice, human rights, and environmental protection. They don't just have a values and mission statement; they have a "values, activism, and mission" statement.[19] Including the word "activism" in a mission statement is something I'd guess not a lot of other companies would dare to do. But for the historic ice cream giant, it fits.

Different as these two organizations may be, they are both well known for their values—and they do a great job of bringing people together around those values. If you want the kind of loyalty that brands like Ben & Jerry's or Chick-fil-A inspire, it's worth looking at values when hiring employees—first, what are your values, and second, do they share those? These questions are even worth considering when you decide what suppliers or vendors to work with.

The values question also applies when hiring part-time staff— which is a great solution if the thought of hiring someone full time makes you nervous. Just start smaller. Over the last five years, I've noticed that hiring has shifted toward hiring "fractional" people. Companies are hiring fractional marketing teams, sales forces, and even administrative support staff. If you aren't ready to hire a full-time individual, you can still hire fractional staff. However, you want to make sure your full-time and part-time staff work well together; if they have shared values, collaboration becomes easier.

Whether they're full or part time, be judicious as you choose that core team of people. Make sure they have values that align with

---

18 "Culture & Values," Chick-fil-A, n.d., accessed September 25, 2023, https://www.chick-fil-a.com/careers/culture.

19 "Our Values, Activism and Mission," Ben & Jerry's, n.d., accessed September 25, 2023, https://www.benjerry.com/values.

your organization's—and, of course, beyond that, you've got to make sure they have the right skills. People have to be able to do the work.

FIND THE RIGHT SKILLS

Often, small business owners become generally aware that they can't manage operations themselves anymore, but they don't do a thorough analysis of what they need done and by whom. This can result in faulty hiring. Before you even post a job ad, there has to be an understanding of the job that you want done so you can accurately evaluate the best possible person to do it.

How do you do that? For solopreneurs or small business owners, one useful question to ask is this: *What are the things that only I can do in the business, and what are the things that someone else can do—or that I would prefer to have someone else do?* If someone showed up here right now, what would you tell them to do? What is the little piece of your world you'd want them to take on? That can be a first step in determining if you need more people—and how many and what for. Just write down a list of all those things.

Then, you have to look at the things that you want someone else to do and delineate between the nonskilled tasks—basically, *stuff I don't want to deal with anymore*—and skilled tasks, basically *stuff I don't feel confident or comfortable doing myself.* You want to get really specific about the gap you have and what needs to be done, whether you simply don't have time for it or you aren't proficient in it. This is how you can start to define the roles you need to hire for, say an administrative assistant versus a bookkeeper.

This process will help you create tightly defined job descriptions so that a specific role aligns with a niche set of skills and strengths. Putting some thought into this process prevents you from hiring a person to do things they aren't qualified for. It also prevents you from hiring someone overqualified to do tasks that another person—less qualified and thus less costly—could do.

Some business owners fall into the trap of bringing on family members only because they are readily available, without considering whether those family members are right for the job. Hiring family may be convenient, at first. Many small business owners hire their family or their kids' friends or someone they know from the neighborhood. In their mind, hiring someone known alleviates the leadership concern of trust. They gain peace of mind with the thought that *I know these are good people because I know them.*

Trust is important, but so is skill. Often, family doesn't have the depth of experience to consistently add value—and that's what you want from your inner circle in business. Value. It starts with finding the right person with the right skills for the job.

In the first chapter I referenced the strong values-based environment at Pinnacle Bank and how the values were reinforced consistently through annual reviews. One of the things that made the company so successful in this regard was hiring based on referrals from existing employees. However, any new hire had to have ten years of specific experience in the role for which they were being hired and in the particular market in which they were to be hired. It takes both values, alignment and skill, to be successful in the hiring game.

I suggest you approach hiring as if you were the human resources head for a Fortune 500 company. Be logical in your choices. Think of a time when you didn't get a job you applied for—there was likely a good reason for it. Maybe you didn't have the experience or the skills or the portfolio of work. Back then, you may not have seen the reason for it; perhaps, in retrospect, you can.

Back in my early career days, I applied for a strategy job at a bank. I was convinced I was extremely well qualified and a great person for the role, so I was surprised when I didn't get it. I remember the feedback that I got was that they were looking for a "heavy hitter." I was really stung at the time. Looking back, I can see that I wasn't a perfect fit. I had a lot to offer—but I also didn't have twenty years of experience under my belt. That's what the company was looking for.

As you start to hire, be honest with yourself. Are you highly selective about who you're bringing on? Are you finding not only the best people but also the best people who align with your mission and values? Are you being judicious about the status of the people that you're bringing on? There is no shame in being picky about who you bring into your business. You should be just as picky about who you allow into your business as you are with who you allow into your home.

> ## 🧪 TO THE LAB!
>
> I've included some resources to help you with hiring in the "In Your Lab" resource section at the conclusion of chapter 4. See the Recruitment Checklist.

CREATE STRONG BONDS

It's not enough to gather an A-plus group of *individuals*. You need to build an A-plus *team* that's bonded and connected to your core—the heart of your business, its mission and vision. It starts with you, the business owner and leader, defining that heart, as David did. You can then build a tightly bonded community around your business. That's how you'll get that densely packed bowling ball of a business you want, the one with the mass needed to withstand external forces.

Businesses may spend a lot of energy hiring but not enough energy to create strong bonds between their people—and between the people and the business's core mission, vision, and values. A simple example is the onboarding process. A small business owner might think onboarding is only for massive corporation. In fact, it's valuable for any company of any size.

Maybe you can remember a job you started where you didn't get a sufficient onboarding experience. You were sitting at your desk on day one when you suddenly realized, *I have no clue how to use this software they want me to use*, or *I don't even know where the toilets are in this place*. Nobody wants to feel that way when they start a new job. Onboarding covers these practicalities. But it's also a chance to address the *bonding* issue and to create connection.

One firm I worked for exceled in this. If you were new to this company, you were greeted on your first day with a welcome sign in the lobby. In that first week, colleagues would come by to introduce themselves personally. You'd have a mentor assigned to explain all the necessary systems and processes to you. You'd receive a personal testimonial from a senior leader. You'd also receive handwritten notes from senior leaders in the company expressing delight in your hire and encouragement to do truly great things for the company.

Later on, you'd be brought together with a larger group of recent hires—people who had joined the organization in the previous months. This group would have the chance to spend three days with the CEO and founder, personally discussing the organization's vision, mission, and values. Then, the senior leader for each part of the company would present about their functional area. As a new worker, seeing that senior leadership was taking the time to welcome you was impactful.

And then came "The Wall."

The company had this giant wall, like you might see on a ropes course or a military training base. It was too big for one person to scale alone. All the new employees would gather at the base of the wall, while a handful of seasoned employees stood at the top of the wall. Between lifting up by fellow new employees and reaching down from veterans, it became apparent that what seemed insurmountable was actually possible. The task required trusting your teammates and working together (and facing some awkward moments)! There would be people who would say they weren't going to climb the wall, that they weren't in good enough physical condition to get to the top. But, in the end, almost everyone went over it. I think in the whole history of the firm, of some two thousand-plus employees they've hired, there's only been a handful that didn't make it to the top of The Wall.

That's a very concrete representation of how coalescing people around a common goal can bring them together. Hitting on the company values of partnership, teamwork, and getting results, the employees found themselves in an experiential dynamic that taught them the lesson in an unforgettable way. That kind of bonding process feeds that entrepreneurial energy we talked about in the first chapter. It also creates trust, something that's increasingly questioned in today's workforce—especially as companies move from on-site to off-site work. Companies are worried about trust, but in my view, what they're really worried about is connections. A lack of connectivity creates a lack of trust.

As a small business owner, you want to know that people are doing their jobs and that they're being productive and adding value to the company. That requires having some level of trust—and that trust is found in connection. A well-thought-out onboarding process is an easy way to take that first step toward connection. An activity like The Wall *bonds* people.

The value of that bond is huge. If we're going to talk physics, it's like the difference between a compound and a mixture. A compound is a pure material that's made up of two or more elements that have been combined. An example would be salt ($NaCl$), which is made up of the elements sodium (Na) and chloride (Cl). If you have a handful of salt, you can't separate the Na and Cl—they're bonded.

Meanwhile, a mixture also brings together different parts—but physical means can still be used to separate those parts. An example would be a handful of jellybeans. You can pick out individual beans. That's great if you're trying to find your favorite flavor. But if you're talking about people in a company, you don't want them to separate so easily. You want the bonding of a compound, not a mixture. Your onboarding can play a big part in that.

If you're looking for more ways to build an engaged workforce, I'd recommend *On Fire at Work: How Great Companies Ignite Passion in Their People without Burning Them Out*, by Eric Chester. It's another book I recommend to many business owners and includes case studies, plus interviews with senior leaders from companies like Ben & Jerry's. If you want to get inspired, it's a great starting point.

CONTINUE TO INVEST IN YOUR NUCLEUS

Of course, onboarding isn't the last stop on the railroad. You have to continue to nurture those bonds and feed trust through regular contact with our team. Even as a small business owner, investing in employee development and growth is worth your while. When you're just getting your business off the ground, for example, you might find that you rarely, if ever, get downtime. Many entrepreneurs don't feel comfortable taking a vacation. But if you had a trusted employee who could run the show while you were away … well, wouldn't that be nice?

What's more, each individual in your organization can become their own generator of energy. If they're folded into your larger vision, with the right values, that energy will be channeled in a way that benefits your organization. This is one point where I again must acknowledge a big difference between the physical world and the business world: every person you bring into your organization will have their own energy—their own molecular vibrations—generated by what they aspire to, which is what energizes them.

Investing in individuals is one way to harness that energy. When you invest in the skills and leadership development of your workers, you are showing them you care about their own growth and aspirations; you're feeding their energy. At the same time, you are building your organization's mass and density by increasing your worker's competence, strength of character (through values reinforcement), and leadership ability. You are helping to craft that heavyweight individual that you want on your team.

Investing in the people who work for you is also simply a way to keep them excited about what they're doing every day. That's how you'll create a positive workforce of good vibes—happy, buzzing molecules who are feeding their energy into your business (and those good vibes can also be felt by your customers).

There's no doubt that investing in your employees—that vital part of your nucleus—is beneficial. Still, small business owners may be worried about the cost and commitment of such an investment. It will be worth it *if you've gotten the other parts of hiring right*. I understand that you don't want to invest big bucks in a worker who's going to quit tomorrow or who isn't contributing mass to your team and isn't well bonded to the organization. Avoid that pitfall by addressing the previous components—defining a clear values-based vision, identifying people who share those values, articulating the skills you need to hire for, and taking steps to bond people together. *Then*, investing in those people will make sense and feel great.

How can you make sure you're on the right track with your employee hiring and management? For small business owners who are managing teams for the first time, this can be a big concern. The answer is simple: consistently solicit feedback from your team members to assess how they're feeling. Are they still connected to the cause? Do they have the tools they need to succeed? Is there a way you can better support them?

Regular one-on-one meetings with your employees can help you answer these questions. Try to use open-ended questions (not yes/no) to get the maximum amount of useful feedback. You can also have employees complete digital surveys, even anonymously, using a tool like SurveyMonkey. By collecting their input, you can make sure your bonds are holding strong—and that you're maintaining that high level of good energy you want in your business.

With regular checks and balances, you can make sure you're getting hiring and team-building right. Both are essential to building a strong company culture. A strong culture will also support a positive work environment that's attractive to top talent. The "best of the best" on the job market know that they deserve the best and won't settle. They're looking for companies that share their values and that are willing to invest in their skills. When you commit to creating a positive work environment, those people will be willing to commit to you and can make up a vital part of your nucleus.

> ### 🜹 TO THE LAB!
>
> I've included some resources to help you assess team bonds in the "In Your Lab" resource section at the conclusion of chapter 4. See the Workplace Environment Survey.

From Your Company to Your Customers: How Your Nucleus Attracts Electrons

As you build your business's team, you are building mass, creating energy and a magnetic field that draw your target clients to your company. In this moment, you are realizing your entrepreneurial vision. That is the entire point of being in business—to fulfill your mission in the most profound way possible. It is the fruition of the entrepreneurial energy we discussed at the outset.

Let's get back to physics and that nucleus I mentioned. If you, the business owner, are the protons, and your employees are the neutrons, you might consider the customers the electrons that buzz around.

Now, a physicist like my friend Marcus will caution me that electrons have practically no mass—they contribute virtually nothing to the mass of an atom. The nucleus of protons and neutrons makes up about 99.9 percent of the atom's mass. We'll give ourselves a little leeway on this point: in the business world, your customers are worth much more than 0.01 percent! They can make or break your business success. The similarity here—and why the analogy stands, at least in my mind—is this: electrons are attracted to the atom's nucleus. The electrons are negatively charged, while the nucleus is positively charged.

So, if you've got that positively charged, dense nucleus, you can count on attracting some excited electrons, also known as your customers. All this adds to your business's mass, which can impact your success in a very real way. When you've got the support of a strong customer base, for example, you have more heft in the marketplace.

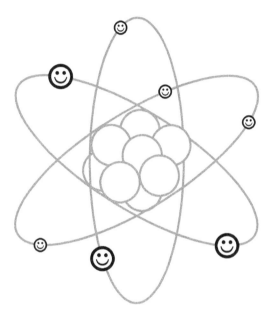

Brand loyalty is a great example. Think about a brand that you like—one that you champion and tell your friends about. Consider brands like SPANX or Specs, for instance. Mac is another example. A lot of people are Apple users for life. Switching to an Android phone or PC computer is simply unthinkable. The success lies in the brand's ability to clearly define a problem that they're on a mission to solve in a creative way. In Apple's case, that means answering the question of how to combine top-tier technological prowess with attractive design.

As a small business owner, how can you win that kind of loyalty and gain that kind of traction? How can you get your electrons, your customers, just as excited about your product or service as you are?

How can you get them *buzzing* around the nucleus of your atom? Again, the answer is pretty simple: talk to your customers!

This is one area where I see small business owners being penny wise and pound foolish—too economical. They aren't investing the time, energy, or money needed to connect with customers. Instead, they just transact with them. Transactions might bring in immediate monetary gain in the short term, but they won't build the lasting bonds and connections needed to sustain brand loyalty in the long term.

John C. Maxwell, whom I've mentioned previously, speaks to this in his book *Everyone Communicates, Few Connect*. Creating connection means going first. This requires energy. You must take the initiative and accept that, between you and your customers, you will inevitably have to take on the role of connector. One way to do that with customers is to create a memorable experience for them—that's usually what hooks people and gets them coming back, whether that memorable experience is above-par customer service or an elite product.

One of my all-time favorite personal stories in this regard is about my family's decision to change to a pickup dry-cleaning service. Up to that point, we had always visited a physical store location. The most critical part of the story is that we have a little fur ball of a dog named Roy, about fifteen pounds, who gets very animated when people come up on our porch. I think it is his way of letting us know he is adding value. After a few iterations with the dry cleaner, I began to notice that the delivery person would leave a dog biscuit for Roy at drop-off and pickup. Roy became so accustomed to that routine that whenever he saw that orange dry-cleaning bag hanging from our front door, he would sit in our foyer and just stare at the front door, knowing that something good was coming. It is usually the little things, isn't it?

On a more technical level, I also want to point out how easy it is to connect with customers with modern technology. It's not like you have to hire an expensive market research firm to run focus groups, like you might have in the past. It's as easy as collecting information via a digital survey tool—again, SurveyMonkey is an economical choice. Or, if you want to go old school, you can even set up a suggestion box in your business. Social media is another wonderful way to connect with consumers at minimal cost.

Initiating conversations with your customers in these ways helps you not only make sure you're meeting their needs but also connects you to them. You are showing them, "Hey, I care about you and your opinion!" That's how you'll create lasting bonds with more people—adding density and mass to your business and, hopefully, making it an unstoppable bowling ball.

🧪 TO THE LAB!

I've included some resources to help you assess your bonds with your customers at the conclusion of chapter 4. See the Client Satisfaction Survey.

Beware: The Greater the Mass, the Greater the Inertia

The holy grail we're working toward in this book is momentum. I've got good news for you: we're almost there. Remember the equation: momentum = mass x velocity. By building your mass and controlling your velocity, you've already done the work needed to achieve momentum! Congratulations; that's a huge accomplishment. In chapter 6, we'll look at what to do when the equation is complete, and you get your momentum.

But before we get to that, there's one more thing we've got to address—inertia. Because here's the thing: the greater an object's mass, the greater its inertia. In physics, inertia is the idea that objects naturally resist any change to their state of motion. That's a good thing when an unwelcome force is enacted on your business that you want to counteract; it helps keep your bowling ball rolling straight for the pins. But inertia also makes it harder to course correct. It's more difficult to shift or pivot a more massive entity than a smaller, more agile one.

The answer isn't minimizing mass, because greater mass gives you momentum—that holy grail we're working toward through this book. But you *do* need to know how to manage inertia. The secret lies in great leadership—something that anyone can learn.

⚗ IN YOUR LAB

This chapter's key business question asked how you can ensure your business is massive enough to easily roll through obstacles without getting derailed. Here are some tools from the Bizzics website to help:

- **Recruitment Checklist:** Use this go-to checklist to ensure you are hiring in a strategic, thoughtful manner.

- **Workplace Environment Survey:** Is your team satisfied on the job? Use this survey to find out.

- **Client Satisfaction Survey:** You want your clients to be happy so they come back again and again—and champion your business to others. Let's find out if they're satisfied.

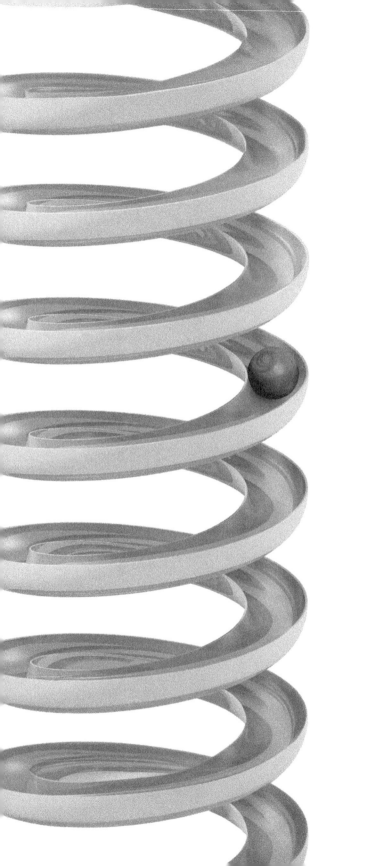

Inertia

My hometown of Nashville is known as Music City. I'm not a musician myself, but I enjoy live music—I'm still hoping to catch Donald Fagen of Steely Dan one day. I'm in awe of these groups of musicians that work together so seamlessly, making it look easy, each on their own instrument. Everyone is doing their own thing, but they all come together to make one great sound.

As much as I love big names and big concerts, one of my favorite musical experiences is songwriter nights. Three or four songwriters gather to play a sampling of their work, usually on stage together, taking turns. Sometimes, you hear directly from the source of a major hit and get to learn the backstory of the song; other times, you hear fresh, new music that might be coming out on a major label soon.

What blows me away every time is how these musicians, who may be meeting each other for the first time, are able to jump into a song and play together without any major preparation. Jazz great Wynton Marsalis describes improvisation like this: "In Jazz, it isn't a matter of making any old thing up. Jazz, like any language, has its own grammar and vocabulary. There's no right or wrong, just some choices that are better than others."[20] When I see musicians on stage at these songwriter nights, it's clear they all speak the same language—music. They only need to hear the first bars of the song to catch the key, tempo, and general vibe. Each does their best to add to the experience and make it memorable for the audience. In the crowd, you never know what is going to happen until the song is a few bars in, which makes it exciting.

In those moments, I'm reminded of the millions of notes these artists have played in their lifetimes. They make those impromptu jam sessions look flawless—because they know exactly what to do in any given situation.

That is exactly the constellation you want for your business. Once the inspiration, organization, and planning we covered in chapters 1 to 3 is complete, it's time to get on stage. It's live action. Everything you do is kinetic, constantly moving. Straight lines are nearly impossible because of all the vector forces, each one with its own wild swings in intensity. To keep up, you want a band of musicians, each capable of operating independently. You can't run between the electric guitar and the bass and the drums and the tambourine and do it all on your own (not if you want a good-sounding song, anyway)!

That's what leadership is. Leadership doesn't mean doing it all yourself. It means inspiring, motivating, and empowering others to act. If you can accomplish that, you'll end up with an organization that is extremely agile—and an agile organization is how you avoid the risks associated with inertia.

---

20   "Supercomputers Help Scientists Tune into Lingo of Jazz Improv," Penn State Institute for Computational and Data Sciences, February 18, 2022, https://www.icds. psu.edu/supercomputers-help-scientists-tune-into-lingo-of-jazz-improv/.

According to the premise of inertia, an object will continue its current motion until some force causes its speed or direction to change. Mass helps your organization counter external forces because it increases inertia. However, greater inertia also has risks: if you want to change the course of your business in any way—perhaps because you need to avoid some sort of collision or move to greater opportunities—you've got to contend with the added resistance of more massive inertia. Things are going to stay the same until you provide some sufficient impulse or stimulus to change them.

That's more easily done when you aren't a one-man band. With great leadership, you empower the other musicians in your group, getting them all to play their own instruments at the same time—the right tune, on key and on tempo. If you have to adapt, say slow down the rhythm a bit, all it will take is a nod to your fellow bandmates for that to happen.

What if you don't have a team because you're a solopreneur? Let me point out, odds are that won't always be the case. Your business is probably going to be bigger than you at some point. When that point comes, already having some idea of how to lead will be invaluable.

Unfortunately, leadership is something I have seen many small business owners struggle with. In some cases, they simply dismiss it. They believe that "leadership" is a muddy concept that only applies to big-business CEOs and isn't relevant to a small mom-and-pop-shop style of business. They assume leadership isn't a big deal if they've got a team of just a few people, which keeps them from exploring the topic altogether. In other cases, small business owners lack the confidence that they can learn leadership. They think they should get a fancy, expensive education or need certain experience to lead.

Here's the secret: leadership skills *can* be learned, and you don't have to go to Harvard to learn them. Putting the effort into leadership development is well worth it, regardless of how many people you're managing. Even if you have just one employee right now, consider giving some care to your leadership development. It will be easier to master leadership behaviors when you're managing a one-person team than, say, a ten- or fifty-person team.

Leadership is also how you get people outside of your organization excited about what you're doing. Great leaders inspire others. That's how you catch the imagination of potential customers, suppliers, investors, and partners. Leadership is about a lot more than just managing direct employees. Done right, it can help contribute to your business's energy and support positive momentum. Let's look at how that's done.

> ## 🔑 KEY BUSINESS QUESTION:
>
> How will you sustain the positive leadership needed to keep your business energized and agile?

Leadership Means Creating Other Leaders

Among countless valuable insights and strategies on leadership he provides, my mentor John C. Maxwell offers two fundamental truths about leadership. First, everything rises and falls on leadership. Second, every leader and every organization has a "leadership lid," a capacity for leadership beyond which their organization cannot grow. John has written over sixty-five books on leadership, a testament to the great breadth and depth of the topic. I can't begin to cover that all—but I do want to present some ideas related to leadership that I believe are relevant to the momentum equation we have been working on.

In the previous chapter, we talked about atoms. Now, atoms are capable of producing huge amounts of energy through fission and fusion. In the fission process, an unstable, heavy nucleus is split into two lighter nuclei. In the fusion process, two light nuclei are combined to create vast amounts of energy.

In the real world, fission is what's used in nuclear reactors to produce power. It works, but it also comes with risks, like nuclear meltdowns. Fusion isn't yet used to produce power, but scientists believe it's possible to do so—and it's an appealing option, because it creates less radioactive material than fission. There's less risk of toxic meltdown.

The traditional hierarchical organizational structure lends itself to the idea of fission. Leadership begins at the top of the organizational chart and is subdivided into smaller sections, which may compete for power, resources, and decision-making rights. Natural toxicities develop among people and units as these daily struggles for control play out. The reality is that you have very few *leaders*—instead, you have lots of managers with low levels of empowerment.

By the time you work your way down to the customer, where decisions need to be made quickly and decisively, the experience is one of frustration and confusion, as people are "checking up the line" for leadership approval. I have seen leaders in this kind of environment, desperate for an energy boost, *create* crises, competitions, and turf battles among units in the hierarchy, leaving those well down in the hierarchy to deal with the toxic side effects.

As a leader, when you invite others to lead as well—when you give them agency—you're taking that *fusion* approach. Instead of separating, you're bonding. You're encouraging other people in your business to go on the entrepreneurial journey with you. In the process, you're giving them some level of control.

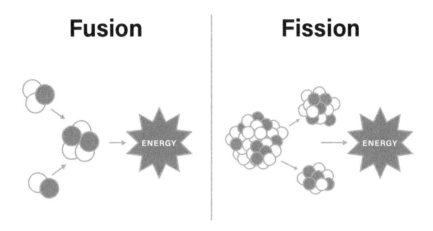

This not only minimizes the risk of toxicity—it also creates energy. This is very valuable, because it's unsustainable for one person to provide the power needed to keep a business's energy high indefinitely. Great leaders allow others to contribute their valuable energy and then channel that energy as needed (for example, toward customers).

This is precisely what we talked about in chapter 1 when we noted that the entrepreneur is both an energy source and energy distributor. The unique *potential energy* present in the power grid is harnessed when you—the entrepreneur—bring people into your grid, keenly aware of each person's possibilities for generating power within that grid. In this context, the term "em*power*ment" suddenly makes a lot of sense.

Again, one of the best examples I've seen of this comes from the Raise the Roof Academy. David and Marlene were intent on solving the problem of poverty in a different way than others before them—through a simple message of "No hero is coming!" Empowerment, self-leadership, and, most importantly, education would win the day. The challenge would be connecting the people that David and Marlene intended to serve with the missional focus of Raise the Roof Academy. This meant inspiring them *and* giving them personal agency.

When I joined the mission team in 2013, we taught leadership principles to roughly one thousand community leaders in an open field. Many of them walked barefoot from thirty to forty miles away, bringing with them enough possessions on their backs to get them through the week. Today, Raise the Roof Academy has slightly more than fifteen hundred students, ninety-four staff, and thirty-six partner schools. They have a brand-new high school campus under construction. Best of all, their students are thriving: 97 percent of students passed the exit exam from primary level 2, the last stop before high school, and their graduates are committed to their dreams of becoming teachers, nurses, engineers, doctors, and more.

Raise the Roof is now a model of education in Uganda. Below, I explain how they did it—by inspiring, motivating, and empowering others. And, just as importantly, through clear communication and building trust.

INSPIRE TO CREATE: TOUCH SOMETHING DEEPLY PERSONAL

It's clear that David's story is unique and a great inspiration. He exemplifies the concept of "pay it forward." Approximately a thousand Raise the Roof students are sponsored, just as David was sponsored in his own difficult life story. The sponsors may never meet the children they help in person, but David and Marlene nurture connections with them through letter-writing campaigns and seasonal gift giving. And those connections inspire generosity.

Inspire is another one of those words, like *momentum*, that is used extensively, especially when great and heroic things are happening. It is worth our time to stop and understand what it really means—literally to breathe into another.[21] I particularly like the translations from some of the old languages like Greek, which add a spiritual dimension to it, conveying an idea of *breathing into another's spirit*. When people recognize something deeply personal in your words and actions, it is life giving. There is some innate shared hopefulness or promise that stirs people's hearts—their spirits. We might even call it a *vibration*.

Part of David's success has come down to his ability to inspire. This began with his personal story, which informs the mission and vision he and Marlene articulated for Raise the Roof. And they didn't just *say* they were going to do these things. They did them, even before the sponsorships started coming in. When they started, they had just one small plot of land, two teachers, and some clapboard, dirt-floor cabins.

At that time, David and Marlene weren't even focused on external partnerships, because their primary focus was getting buy-in from the community. That's where the inspiration had to start—that was where they'd start building their mass. David wanted to make sure that the community trusted him and understood his vision, so he invited them to join forces with him. He connected with community leaders and brought them into the process, uniting them around his vision. And it worked—like I said, that first invitation, the initial leadership training, saw some one thousand people coming to participate, some of them walking up to forty miles to be there. David and Marlene's vision became personal to all.

This was no small feat, especially given the conditions of the area at that time. Many communities had been ravaged by HIV/AIDS, and alcoholism was rampant, particularly among men. The name Bwassandeku means "broken jar," a reference to the high level of alcoholism

---

21   "Breathing Life into 'Inspire,'" *Merriam-Webster*, n.d., accessed September 25, 2021, https://www.merriam-webster.com/wordplay/the-origins-of-inspire.

in the area. A lot of people were on simple survival mode—building their own houses with mud bricks from their yards, sharecropping, and just getting by.

David's message was, essentially, "Things here can be different to the extent that you want to make them different." A large part of Raise the Roof's initial messaging was devoted to this self-empowerment and the emphasis that this wasn't about inviting in foreigners to drive the bus—but to get the community driving the bus itself. That is the kind of inspirational messaging that makes people want to act because it's giving them the permission to act. It's encouraging them to take the wheel.

Such messages especially resonated with parents. As a father of three myself—and having interacted with literally thousands of other parents through the neighborhood, schools, Boy Scouts, sports, and religious life over the years—I do not know of anything more deeply personal than the hopes and dreams we have for children. Generational improvement is the dream of any parent, whether that means better health, financial security, or simply magnifying their children's gifts for the betterment of others. That idea just stirs people's hearts. Again: It inspires.

A lot of small business owners can learn from David and how he inspires others. Now, you might be thinking, "My business is just selling a product. It's not doing something like building schools in Uganda! How can I compare?"

The premise is the same. When you have a strong vision and then you invite people to take part in realizing that vision, that's exciting for them. That energizes them. People start thinking about what they can personally become in the context of what you're inviting them to create with you. They'll rise to the occasion and take action—and they'll also allow themselves to be creative.

Some people think that creativity doesn't have a space in the strict world of business, but I don't think that's true. Most great businesses have creativity at their core. In the same way, people might not think of physics as a creative field. After all, it's full of rules and laws. But keep in mind that physics governs the natural world around us, and what a wonderful creative force *that* is. From the perfect snowflake to the seasons, nature is full of creative wonders. Similarly, you can make space for creative wonders in your business by fostering creativity in individuals. If you're always squashing people's attempts to be creative—or to make a simple decision—you're going to lose out on great business ideas. By inviting cocreators into your business, you avoid the trap of "that's the way we have always done things" and encourage innovation.

I think the creativity of humans is innate—not the artistry, necessarily, but the desire to make new things, and fix and change things.

By inspiring your employees, you're building that entrepreneurial energy in them too.

When you're inspiring people, it's almost like a way of ensuring that you're never going to be a part of the status quo. Because people are finding the best of themselves in the context of what you're trying to do, and then they'll identify opportunities. They'll find new and different ways of doing things. By inspiring your employees, you're building that entrepreneurial energy in them too—and that benefits them and you alike.

As a small business owner, how can you inspire? Articulate that vision and mission, again and again. Just as importantly, lead by example. Espouse the values encapsulated in your mission and vision, and act on them. Show that they aren't just words.

MOTIVATE TO JOIN AND MOVE WITH YOU

Inspiring people is a useful first step in motivating them to act. Still, there can be a gap between inspiration and motivation—one that great leadership knows how to close. Here, credibility can play a big part. Don't just *say* something; back it up with something tangible. Show them what to do!

Again, I can look to my friends David and Marlene for inspiration on this point. David and Marlene knew that if they wanted to motivate both community support and financial sponsorship, credibility was a must. This began with the Raise the Roof faculty and staff. They started with two teachers who had limited experience but still enough to be effective with the youngest students.

Then, they entered a prolonged upgrade mode as the student population aged and grew in numbers, recruiting seasoned educators and headmasters from as far away as Jinja, Uganda's second-largest city and a four-hour drive from Bwassandeku. These educators understood David and Marlene's intention of solving the problem of generational poverty and connected with their unique vision, one rooted in self-empowerment. It was a way of doing things that combined academic education with a way of being in the world that rested on self-leadership.

People could see that this was the real deal. The inspirational vision and mission weren't just big talk. They were backed up with credible, tangible actions—in this case, hiring skilled educators. That's when their support started growing. Motivation grew to support Raise the Roof. In turn, this show of support motivated David and Marlene to do even more; more teachers were hired and more students sponsored. The classroom expanded. Again, we can see how energy spreads.

To me, this is motivation done right. It is motivation rooted in inspiration and backed by credible actions. It's the exact opposite of a toxic environment. I've found that toxic environments—the kinds driven by fission, not fusion—are often informed by fear-based motivation. There's an aura of "Do this or your job is on the line." This is not how people thrive.

As a small business owner, you'll rarely get the best out of others if you're forcing something on them. You won't get that buzzy, inspired, creative, high-vibrational energy you're looking for. You'll probably just get the bare minimum. How we treat each other is the leading indicator of how we treat our customers. In the South we like to say, "Go love on somebody."

So, how are you supposed to motivate? Be a hands-on leader. Be willing to get your hands dirty. Others will take notice. And then, when your team sees you moving forward, they'll hopefully say, "Hey, that's pretty cool. I want to be a part of that too." And they'll join you.

EMPOWER TO ACT

Inspiring and motivating others is the lead up to empowering them, giving them the agency to act of their own accord. This is where you can really start to gain momentum. At the same time, it's how you can more easily manage inertia. Like I said, you can't play every instrument in the band yourself. You want to make sure each person's instrument is tuned to your key and then let them play it themselves.

In David and Marlene's case, empowering local community members proved to be the key to unlocking Raise the Roof's momentum. David and Marlene faced an interesting power structure in Bwassandeku and the surrounding villages. Each community included an influential pastor, always male, and underneath him, the real power structure of the community—the women. The women who had birthed the children the school was for had intense hope for a different kind of future for them. They had an innate personal passion for the initiative. The question was, how to empower them?

David established four zones to connect with the male pastors as well as eleven community centers, led by the most influential women in the community. This allowed Raise the Roof to create deeper connections with the heavy hitters of the region, people who could propel the vision of Raise the Roof forward in smaller clusters in meaningful ways. Empowerment was the key.

From what I've seen in my own experience in business, things tend to move more quickly and consistently in empowered organizations. Businesses that give their workers some control are more agile and innovative. In Michael Gerber's *The E-Myth Revisited*, he offers a disheartening vignette of Sarah, the baker, who has basically taken on every aspect of work in her own small bakery—which has left her overworked and, as a result, unmotivated and uninspired.

This isn't where any entrepreneur wants to end up! Unfortunately, I think there's a danger of that happening in almost any small business. When you don't have empowerment, it's hard to move forward.

Maybe you've worked for a company that doesn't empower its employees. It's the kind of place where, if you want to get anything done, you have to ask your supervisor—and then maybe they have to ask *their* supervisor, who has to check with accounting or HR or whatever the case may be. There's a lot of talk of "That's not my paygrade/responsibility/job. Go talk to this person instead." It can be a really disheartening environment to work in. After a while, you stop trying to take any kind of initiative, because it's too tedious. Ultimately, you might lose your motivation altogether. That's certainly not what you want from your company.

Empowerment is all about human potential and what people are able to do. As a leader, you have to think about not only yourself but also the entire system. You start with your own entrepreneurial energy—you're bouncing back and forth between your current state and your future vision. As people join your organization, you share that energy with them. You get them excited about the vision, energizing them around the common goal.

You begin a long and steady process of *fusion*, bonding people so strongly to your vision, mission, and values that they become one with it. This produces an improvisational culture that rises and falls almost rhythmically in the live performance of your business. The process requires persistent messaging and demonstration by you, the leader, of everything you declare your business stands for.

That kind of combined energy can be very powerful. Look at how energy can be harnessed in the physical world for inspiration. Sustainable energy is a global theme with myriad potential solutions. One of those is replicating solar fusion for commercial use. The US Department of Energy has a flagship laser facility, the SLAC National Accelerator Laboratory, in Menlo Park, California. In 2021, they broke a record when they produced ten quadrillion watts of fusion power for a fraction of a second.[22] That's seven hundred times the generating power of the entire US electrical grid. How did they do it? They trained 192 of the world's highest-energy lasers on a tiny target the size of a peppercorn, filled with hydrogen atoms. The lasers were magnified through a series of mirrors to produce the result. Essentially, they recreated the sun on earth.

---

22 Tom Metcalfe, "Fusion Experiment Breaks Record, Blasts Out 10 Quadrillion Watts of Power," Live Science, August 18, 2021, https://www.livescience.com/fusion-experiment-record-breaking-energy.html.

Imagine if you could get all your employees in on the peppercorn of your business—what a lot of entrepreneurial energy that would create! The leader is the laser, fixed on that peppercorn of employees. My former CEO who spent three solid days with every new employee is a great example of a lasered-in leader. You don't need a fancy lab in Menlo Park to do the same. You can do it in your own "lab," your business. Empowerment is the answer.

Empowerment begins with hiring, which we talked about in the previous chapter. When you've got the right people with fitting values and skills, you have a great deal of potential energy at your fingertips. It's then on you, the business leader, to get the ball rolling and nudge each individual's potential into kinetic energy.

Assign those team members clear roles and responsibilities, and trust them to act. Individuals in the business can then move toward the larger goal in a way that's energized and agile. Empowerment is the ultimate advantage in agility. It allows you to operate in a fluid environment, with people at all levels of the organization noticing things and taking appropriate action as swiftly as possible. That's the good news.

The bad news? In my experience, empowerment is the most difficult of the three points we've discussed here—inspiration, motivation, and empowerment. Why? No business owner enjoys losing control over what they have built, and empowerment has inherent risks that must be managed with appropriate authority. For example, in banking, new lenders receive only a fraction of the lending authority of senior people. Limitations like these can help organizations empower individuals safely.

At the same time, for empowerment to work, you must have a growth mindset toward people—one that accommodates mistakes as learning opportunities. Yes, I said mistakes! They will happen. You will make them. Your employees will make them too. Remember, this is how experience is built, and experience makes your people stronger.

It takes time, and mistakes will happen. That said, when you build a culture of trust and empowerment, you end up with an organization where people have the ability to respond and make decisions, without getting bogged down in hierarchy or procedure. You end up with agility.

> ## 🧪 TO THE LAB!
>
> I've included some resources to help you empower others in the "In Your Lab" resource section at the conclusion of chapter 5. See the Empowerment Template.

COMMUNICATE TO CONNECT

Inspiring others, motivating them, and empowering them—it starts with and depends almost entirely on communication. Small business owners often struggle with communication skills. Part of it just comes down to a lack of experience. In other cases, people assume there isn't much need for grand communication in a small team.

Unfortunately, failing to communicate can threaten the density of your organization: you risk losing those valuable bonds that contribute to your mass. Even if you're a small team—perhaps, especially if you're a small team—those bonds are so important and need to be nurtured.

I spoke about this briefly in the first chapter, when we discussed building out your power grid and sharing your entrepreneurial energy with others. Communication is a key component of this. You want to pay attention to all forms of communication: visual, nonvisual, spoken, and unspoken. This reflects back to the basics of espousing your business's values. Are you talking the talk *and* walking the walk? That's how you both inspire and motivate. Good communication skills also benefit your business in other ways. Knowing how to talk to potential suppliers, partners, investors, and lenders will help you approach these conversations with confidence.

But communicating is not connecting, and connecting is what we are after if we desire a fusion-based leadership model with great agility. Standing in that gap between communicating and connection is *listening*. Active listening shows that you're respecting others' opinions, which plays to the empowerment piece of the puzzle. This is again an area where we can learn from David and Marlene.

When they introduced the concept of Raise the Roof to the community, it wasn't in a top-down way. They invited opinions, thoughts, and ideas—even if they weren't directly related to education. The feedback they got was astounding.

Once people in the community recognized David and Marlene's commitment, they really wanted to figure out what *they* could do to make the community better, especially economically. The initiative went well beyond schooling. David and Marlene started meeting with local small businesspeople, mostly women, to discuss the possibilities. They were introducing new ideas beyond schooling that might better the community, like animal husbandry, tailoring, and construction.

By allowing for that level of dialogue, Raise the Roof was able to have a much greater influence. It became a community-building exercise, one with economic impact stretching far beyond the initial point that David had picked of building a schoolhouse. That's the kind of power you get from good communication. How can you harness it for yourself?

Just like leadership, communication can be learned. I often recommend one of John C. Maxwell's books, *Everyone Communicates, Few Connect*. It's a wonderful resource that focuses on not only building bridges but also bonding with others. There's a bit of a science to how you connect with people, touching on everything from the words you use to your tone, body language, and proximity to them. Maxwell's book covers a lot of useful ground.

Everyone Communicates, Few Connect also helps illuminate some of the markers that show whether you've simply communicated versus connected with someone. Connection is seen when people are responding and co-collaborating—when you can see their sincere energy and interest. I don't want to regurgitate that book here, but I do recommend it to any small business owner hoping to lead better.

⚗ TO THE LAB!

I've included some resources to help you communicate in the "In Your Lab" resource section at the conclusion of chapter 5. See the Communications Checklist and Active Listening Checklist.

MAINTAIN CONSISTENCY TO BUILD TRUST

Trust is an asset that small business owners can use to their advantage—but not all do so. As an entrepreneur, you have a unique chance to connect with the community that supports your business, from suppliers to customers. Even if you're running an online business, you can still connect and create lasting, trusting bonds with your supporters through social media. This gives you a unique edge over big corporations, where people are dealing with faceless individuals. Make the most of it.

Part of building trust comes from the things we've talked about above—inspiring, motivating, empowering, and communicating with others. There's also a reliability aspect. That could mean consistently delivering good quality to your customers, for example, or being consistent in how you compensate and review your employees. When you're consistent, you're giving people permission to trust in you.

Again, Raise the Roof demonstrates the value of consistency in building trust. From the start, David and Marlene made it clear that their educational initiative was for the entire community, regardless of differences like religion. This was a big deal. Externally, they faced divisions among Catholics, Protestants, and Muslims in the community, each in a way wanting to claim the effort of Raise the Roof for *their* people. Religion seemed to drive hard divisions. David and Marlene made a strong statement, and they stood by that statement consistently: age, gender, tribe, faith, or history should not exclude you from opportunity. All are welcome. They then continuously articulated that value and backed it up with their actions. That's how trust was won.

As a small business owner, you can do the same. In the big picture, it all comes back to staying true to your mission and vision. You don't want to suddenly renege and pull the rug out from under people. That won't build trust. But if you stick to your values and emulate them, in speech and action, you'll show people you're worth trusting.

That trust is also how you combat those hierarchical structures I mentioned earlier in the chapter. David and Marlene are a testament to how much work it takes to create a fusion-based leadership system, one that's based on unity and not hierarchy. They have dealt with everything from employee theft to self-interested dealmaking at the expense of Raise the Roof Academy—plus all kinds of other behaviors that did not fit the organization's vision and values. However, they didn't let these setbacks keep them from pursuing a culture of empowerment in the organization.

Whenever an issue raised its head, they always came back to the organization's mission and values, reiterating, "This is not in line with our values. We do not do this." They consistently communicated their vision and values, and maintained excitement about their mission, while inspiring, motivating, and empowering others. Ten years later, this has given them an organization that runs effectively, even when they are thousands of miles away. Raise the Roof Academy is an empowered, agile organization that's able to adjust to new realities quickly—realities that could otherwise throw it off course.

From Inertia to Momentum

You want your business to be a rocket. But when you shoot off a rocket, it's only on its original course about 5 percent of the time. The other 95 percent of the time is about minute adjustments, whether they're ones you're proactively making or reactions to external forces. This is why agility is such a hot topic for entrepreneurs.

If you take the time to inspire, motivate, and empower your team, you can end up with an extremely agile organization, one that has an easier time avoiding collisions. This becomes especially important as your organization gains momentum. This is what all business owners want—and what I hope for you too.

Like inertia, momentum is dependent in part on an object's mass. The more mass an object has, the greater its momentum. Remember: momentum = mass x velocity. Throughout this book, we've been talking about the things that will help your business gain mass:

- Establishing your entrepreneurial energy and creating a clear vision for your business (chapter 1);

- Pointing your business in the right direction with the appropriate velocity (chapter 2);

- Preparing to deal with the forces that may impact your business (chapter 3);

- Drawing in other people to add to that mass (chapter 4); and

- Learning how to lead in a way that allows you to maintain mass while navigating the potential dangers of inertia (chapter 5).

Now, we're finally to that holy grail I keep promising: momentum. Let's look at how to bring it into your business in a sustainable way.

🧪 IN YOUR LAB

At the start of this chapter, I asked you, "How will you sustain the positive leadership needed to keep your business energized and agile?" These resources from the Bizzics website can help:

Empowerment Template: Crack the code to empowering those around you and keeping their vibrational energy buzzing.

Communications Checklist: Make sure you're communicating in a constructive way.

Active Listening Checklist: Ensure you're getting feedback from others in a meaningful manner. Are you really hearing what they're saying?

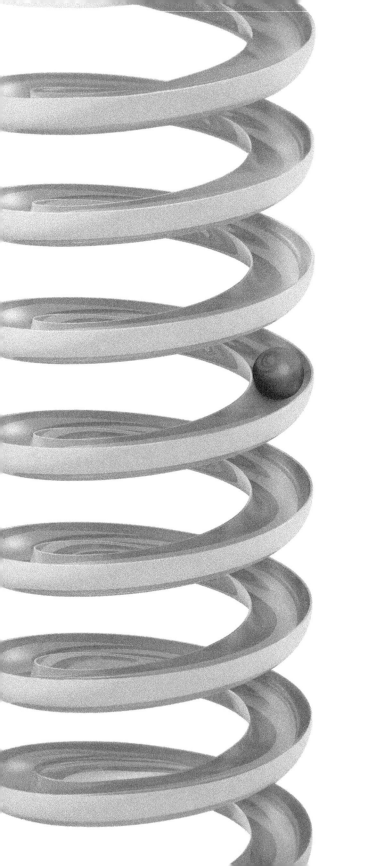

CHAPTER 6

Momentum

A friend of mine, Dennis, owned a short-line railroad. He was always telling me crazy stories about the work, and to this day I think of him whenever I see a freight train. The railroad is actually a very dangerous place to work, and the industry sees a fair number of accidents every year, some of them deadly and, in a few cases, devastating to entire communities. For that reason, Dennis was freakishly concerned about safety, hyperaware of the speed and the mass of what he was hauling at all times. There were curves in the rail line to navigate, along with crossings and unexpected junk lying on the track—the leftovers of storms, vandals, or wiseguys.

My conversations with Dennis were the first time I really thought about the dangers of momentum (even though I had experienced the risks plenty of times as a kid—on my bike, skateboard, and sled). The way Dennis caught my attention was to ask me how long I thought it would take to stop a unit coal train moving at thirty-five miles per hour. A unit coal train consists of 135 cars and weighs approximately nineteen thousand tons in total. Can you guess the answer? I had no idea and was flabbergasted when Dennis told me it would take *miles*.

As with Dennis's railroad, in business we have to be constantly vigilant about the mass we have accumulated and the speed at which we are moving—because we know that there will be curves and unexpected obstacles in our path that could easily derail everything we have built.

Momentum is that holy grail business owners all aspire to. You hear the term used a lot in the corporate world. A company wants to "gain momentum" or "maintain momentum." In business speak, people usually conflate momentum with speed or progress. But it's not quite that simple. You already know what I'm going to say: let's look to physics for a deeper understanding of momentum and what it can mean for your business.

In physics, momentum is defined by the equation mass times velocity. In chapter 2, we discussed velocity, which determines the direction, distance, and speed that your business goes—or, rather, *grows*. If you don't channel the energy and speed of your velocity in a linear direction, you risk your business getting stuck like that pinwheel firework I described: spinning wildly and making a lot of heat and energy, but not actually *going* anywhere. That's a huge waste of that valuable energy we talked about in chapter 1. To avoid that pitfall, you've got to define a business direction—for example, with a strategic framework based on market share, client retention, and profitability, which we laid out in chapter 2.

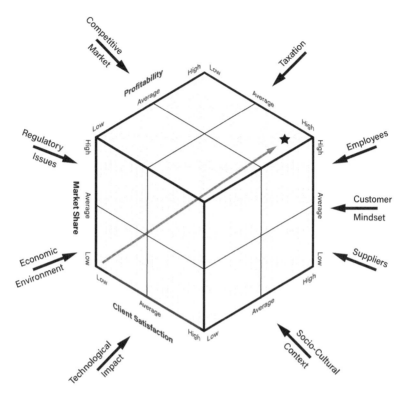

Setting that velocity for your business helps it remain resistant to external forces that might otherwise derail you. Mass also helps your business stay on track, as we've discussed. In physics, mass is a fundamental property of all matter, referring to an object's resistance to the application of force. The greater the mass, the more force is needed to change an object's speed, position, or direction. In business, building mass means coalescing others around the core of your business, its values, in a meaningful way—*bonding* them to your mission and vision.

If you've gotten that velocity part right and you've built mass, you'll be able to gain great momentum for your business. This is the big payoff for putting in all the work outlined in the previous chapters—articulating a business plan, creating a unique selling proposition, building a great culture, hiring the best people, bonding with your clients, and so forth. Momentum is the ultimate reward, with the clear benefits of rolling over nuisance obstacles and competitors alike. Everything seems easy when you have momentum.

The question now is this: How do you sustain that momentum while also regulating it? Wise business owners seem to know when turbulent or uncertain times are coming and throttle back accordingly. I have seen it in both velocity and mass—downsizing and even spinning off divisions and related businesses. Part of that is about monitoring those vectors we touched on in chapter 3; for example, in the banking sector, we know tough times are ahead when builders stop buying lots for home building. Every industry has its own leading indicators.

Regardless of external forces, you want to keep that freight train clicking along, without getting out of control. This is all about remaining competitive in the marketplace. How are you planning to stay on the train tracks so you can get to the place where you want to be—say, to achieve the size of the client base you want, to build the team of heavy hitters you want, or to ensure that your USP is *still* a USP, a strong entry in the market that's unique and differentiated from what others are offering?

There are things that may slow you down and interfere with your momentum—things that cause friction, which I'll talk about more in the next chapter. For now, I don't want to focus on the things you might have to be reactive to; I want to focus on the things that you can proactively do to maintain your momentum. Let's talk about it.

🔑 **KEY BUSINESS QUESTION:**

What actions are you taking to ensure momentum toward your business's goals? How are you identifying and removing the forces that might slow you down?

Momentum Requires Consistency over Time

Momentum is largely about sustaining your business's energy. Sometimes entrepreneurs overlook the fact that the huge energy push required at launch must be followed by consistent energy pushes to keep moving. Once momentum is lost, it's very hard to regain. That doesn't mean you have to constantly exert a huge amount of force to push your business ahead. Force can be applied all at once or in smaller pushes consistently over time. They add up to the same force eventually.

But energy feeds the basic formula: mass times velocity. Consistency requires the discipline of paying attention to this formula in the context of *everything* you see and adjusting accordingly. Velocity is the most manageable variable: if you want to double your velocity, your energy input has to *quadruple*. That also works in reverse, if you're trying to slow down. Depending on your objective, your presence in business may vary.

Further, in the most practical sense possible, velocity will be controlled by the time frames you establish to achieve strategic goals. Remember, velocity incorporates speed, direction, and distance—and you control all of that. Consistency comes from studying it *all the time* and setting objectives accordingly.

Mass is much trickier and often unpleasant to manage, but well worth the effort; it is exhilarating to know that you have built a team that simply cannot be beaten. In the best case, you find yourself constantly upgrading the talent on your team and working to build unbreakable bonds among employees. I enjoy a heavyweight hire with the best of them, but I also know that there is nothing more gratifying than watching an individual grow their skills, personal character and values, and leadership ability.

That said, some people don't share that desire for growth. In those instances, you may need to make staffing changes to create greater density. It can be difficult to be objective when strong human connections have been formed—but it's a must for businesses to survive. I have seen cases where one person can do the work of two, a clear example of trading off size for density (and agility).

In the worst case—if you are confronted by strong adverse vectors in the economy or in your industry—you may have to unpack your team and downsize to survive. Unpacking everything you have bonded to your life's dream is gut wrenching for most business owners, so much so that it creates a tentativeness in hiring even when times are good. In down times, businesses often take the approach of "let's slow down and see if we can get through it before letting anyone go." However, downsizings are often impossible to avoid—and exiting entire businesses that are no longer profitable or relevant to your strategy is equally stressful. No one wants to be disadvantaged by short-term decisions when the market comes roaring back.

Over the past twenty years, I have not seen any industry more challenged to maintain consistency in both velocity *and* mass than the residential mortgage industry. It has been boom or bust, either because of the rate environment or the runaway imbalances in supply and demand that drove the economic crisis of 2007 to 2008. Hopefully your industry is nowhere near as chaotic.

Before we leave the topic of consistency, I want to offer an illustration of the momentum equation that should provide great hope for you as a small business owner. The greater your business's mass *or* the greater its velocity, the greater the momentum you'll get out of it. So, you could have something that's very large (with great mass) that's moving very slowly (with low velocity) and that could have the equivalent momentum of something that's very small (small mass) but moving very fast (high velocity).

Now, if you're a small business owner, you've got to realize that your mass is relatively tiny compared to the big players in the market. You do not have the sheer number of people of a major corporation. That does *not* mean that you can't achieve great momentum. You can have just as much momentum as the big dogs—it just means fine-tuning other parts of the equation, in this case your velocity, even more carefully.

Take a look back at the equation: momentum = mass x velocity. Say you've got a huge amount of mass (1,000 kg), but a small amount of velocity (5 meters/second/north):

Momentum = mass x velocity = 1,000 kg x 5 m/s/north = 5,000 kg meters/second north

Now, say you've got a huge amount of velocity (1,000 meters/second/north), but not a lot of mass (5 kg):

Momentum = mass x velocity = 5 kg x 1,000 m/s/north = 5,000 kg meters/second/north

You get the same result, whichever way the equation plays out. In today's economy, *disruption* seems to be one of the most popular buzzwords. To me, this *is* the formula for disruption, mostly having to do with small, agile firms moving at great speeds toward something new and different.

However, disruption has a lot to do with carving out a specific destination, a segment of business that sees no movement among monolithic business giants—those companies that have gotten large but not gained density. They often operate within hierarchical fission-leadership structure, with lots of managers and bureaucrats. That creates an opening for the small business owner like yourself.

To me, the ideal "entrepreneurial equation" comes from having an agile organization with highly qualified people going after a carefully targeted market. In my forty-plus years of experience, I've found that to be the sweet spot for most entrepreneurs. And I've given you examples of these individuals. Think of Music City Disposal with their neighborhood-by-neighborhood expansion strategy—or Charlie Irwin, who started his painting company, CIP, going door to door, pursuing a one-house-at-a-time expansion strategy.

I have another example right here from my hometown: Emma, a Nashville-based start-up that was bootstrapped by the owners and founded in 2003. Emma offered a software-based marketing solution for a unique targeted audience, providing branded email marketing for businesses. The technology market is infamously cutthroat, and Emma came to fruition at a time when a lot of players were entering the field. How did they stand out? They had a very well-made product that hit the trifecta: technically sound, graphically appealing, and user friendly.

The company didn't *just* have a great product, though. They also nurtured a wonderful culture of innovation and empowerment. Case in point: They were consistently recognized as a top employer in the community.[23] Despite the fast-evolving tech market of the early 2000s, Emma managed to avoid inertia and gain (controlled) momentum. Email evolved rapidly during that time. Think of the rapid addition of new features, from attachments to embedded graphics and hyperlinks—plus the need to fortify against malicious factors like viruses. Emma's amazing team managed to navigate all that chaos. The end result? They sold to a New York venture capital firm for a pretty penny in 2017.[24]

All these small businesses had unique value to add, and they precisely targeted who they were offering that value to. Then, they tapped into their energy to scale up, carefully marshaling their resources to grow without falling victim to hypergrowth. And those companies are still doing great business today.

That's how you sustain that valuable entrepreneurial energy over a long time. You don't want to light the firework of your business and then burn out too quickly. Keep your approach steady and sustained—and keep your energy high by tapping into your resources, especially other people. Remember, other people can bring energy to your business and help you keep it on course. Look at the example of Raise the Roof Academy, which I talked about in the previous chapter; the entire initiative started with David's personal story, but now so many people are involved in realizing his vision.

When you give your careful attention to all these components— velocity, force, mass, inertia—you can create great momentum for

23   Jeff Bradford and Erin Gagnon, "Email Marketing Company Emma Named Top Small Company Workplace by *Inc. Magazine* and Winning Workplaces," Cision, May 27, 2011, https://news.cision.com/emma--myemma-com/r/email-marketing-company-emma-named-top-small-company-workplace-by-inc--magazine-and-winning-workplaces,g9128564.

24   Joel Stinnett, "Nashville Tech Darling Emma Sold, CEO Stepping Down," *Nashville Business Journal*, October 10, 2017, https://www.bizjournals.com/nashville/news/2017/10/10/nashville-tech-darling-emma-sold-ceo-stepping-down.html.

your business. This will help you hold up even against much bigger and better-established competitors. Your mom-and-pop coffee shop *can* compete with Starbucks. Your online clothing store *can* survive alongside Walmart and Target and H&M. Your private software development company *can* thrive in the same marketplace as Microsoft. Those aren't insurmountable competitors. With the right attention, you can take on any Harvard Business School, venture capital–funded cash cow.

But: It's a constant process!

This is so important to me, I've got to say it again: *it is a constant process!* I have unfortunately seen business owners assume that their business is on autopilot, neglect to give it the ongoing care it needs—and then be surprised when it flames out. Throughout this book, I've compared your business to a car, a plane, and a train. Whatever vehicle you want to compare your business to, you've got to make sure you're controlling it.

Maintaining momentum for your business means consistently working on moving forward and remaining dynamic.

Maintaining momentum for your business means consistently working on moving forward and remaining dynamic. You can't write your business plan once, open your business's doors, and hope things are going to go in the direction you want them to. You need to be consistently revisiting all those things you set up that got your business on the right track in the first place. Here are some of the components you'll need to pay attention to.

REVISIT YOUR INITIAL STRATEGY: BUSINESS PLANNING

Remember that business plan we talked about way back in the second chapter? I told you then, business planning isn't a onetime process.

I shared the story of the bank I worked at where, after our annual strategic planning session, the gentleman in charge would always say, "Well, what we have here is the perfect plan." That always made us chuckle, because we knew there was no such thing. The "perfect" plan might remain that way if the business operated in a closed environment, separate from all the influences of the world—recessions, new competitors on the market, global events like pandemics and wars. But businesses don't work that way.

Your business plan requires ongoing evaluation of where your business is currently and where it's going in the future. I recommend small business owners redraft their business plan every year to encompass a new three-year plan. If some earth-shattering event happens—say, the legislative environment around your business changes suddenly—you may need to unexpectedly revisit your plan sooner. The clear-eyed evaluation of vector forces we referenced in chapter 3 is essential and will drive you to or from places in your industry that inertia may otherwise have thwarted. It is not a theoretical exercise.

There's a common assumption that companies that have stood the test of time have done so because they stick to a great idea that they do well. Sometimes that's true; Coca-Cola is one example. But there are also long-standing companies that have adapted to the changing world over time—and *that* has been the secret to their longevity. Nintendo is one example. Nintendo has been around since well before the era of mass-produced video games. They once sold everything from vacuum cleaners to playing cards—and even instant rice. It wasn't until the 1960s that the company found their sweet spot and started producing electronic games. I cannot even begin to imagine how many iterations their business plan had to go through to get there.

> ## 🧪 TO THE LAB!
>
> Is it time to revisit your business plan? See the "In Your Lab" resource section at the conclusion of chapter 6 for a template.

ALWAYS KNOW YOUR VALUE: CONSTANT COMPETITOR ANALYSIS

One of the things that will change the most frequently around your business is the competition. You don't just have to think of the old-timers in the market, the big corporations that seem like the biggest challenge. A young, agile start-up with innovative ideas and a great vision can be just as big a threat. You want to keep an eye on the market and make sure your USP is still just that, a *unique* selling proposition. Keeping an eye on the competition also allows you to stay on top of trends that might influence your customers' demands.

I do not know of an industry that is more faddish or subject to start-up competitors and fast followers than the food industry. Everyone has a different way of doing their staple items and executing the dining experience. In the South, pork seems to be the dish that everyone does one way or another. Everyone has their own way and "secret sauce."

My favorite food trend here in Nashville is the hot chicken craze, if only for the legendary, possibly mythical, origins of industry pacesetter Prince's Hot Chicken—which purportedly started when Mrs. Prince suspected her husband of being unfaithful and stirred up a hot sauce designed to punish him. At the moment of truth in her diabolical plot, her husband licked his lips and said, "Mmm, that's good!" They are now in their fourth generation of ownership, and we have hot chicken places all over Nashville. It's not easy to maintain a business over four generations, so their success comes down to much more than those legendary origins.

What I notice about the food industry is that the great operators never stop testing other people's food and innovating in their own kitchens to get the competitive edge locally. The great restaurateurs I know travel constantly—regionally, nationally, even globally—to see what others are doing that could work for them and to assess potential challenges. It's like a modern-day Marco Polo. I know Nashville's food scene has benefited greatly from the competitive environment. One last thing I love about the food industry is the way that food trucks serve as business incubators of sorts. I have cheered on several operators as they have moved from food truck to stand-alone brick-and-mortar restaurant. In their case, their "business lab" was a truck.

⚗ TO THE LAB!

Are you keeping up with the changing competitive landscape? I include some resources to help you make sure in the "In Your Lab" resource section at the conclusion of chapter 6. See the SWOT Analysis, Competitive Advantage Plan, and Competitor Analysis Template.

CONTINUALLY ARTICULATE YOUR VALUE: SMART MARKETING AND PROMOTION

As your business evolves, you want to make sure you're maintaining mass. That means bringing the people who have coalesced around your business, from employees to customers, with you on the journey. Marketing and promotion are part of that. A lot of people assume "marketing and promotion" is just transactional—the end goal is to get people to purchase your product or service. Really, great marketing and promotion is about creating connections. Yes, those connections may lead to transactions. But the connections need to be rooted in emotion. Marketing and promotion allows you to articulate your value *and* to create bonds. We can never stop reaffirming the purchase decision at the most emotional level possible.

Nike is a great example. The company has always highlighted their USP. Starting with the waffle sole on the shoe, which later became the "air sole," Nike was founded as a company by athletes *for* athletes. They show their product's value clearly in their marketing materials. But they also have an emotional component to their marketing. The "Just Do It" campaign isn't just for athletes. It's an emotional call for any person who feels like they have some challenge to overcome (which is everyone in the world)! And then you couple that emotional call with inspirational figures, like athletes from Cristiano Ronaldo to Serena Williams, and it's no wonder the Nike brand has had such an impact over the years. Nike made their clientele believe that they, too, were competitors and champions, no matter what level they competed on.

The great thing about small businesses is that they do not need multimillion-dollar advertising campaigns to reaffirm purchase decisions. Often, this can be done in person. I'm constantly reminded of my favorite coffee house, the Good Cup, just a couple of miles from our home. Since the restaurant's founding twenty years ago, the ownership has never lost sight of the fact that, while coffee is the commodity, what they are *really* supplying to people is a sense of community. They welcome all who enter their doors, and many connections have been forged here. Just recently, I attended a twenty-year anniversary concert in their parking lot, which was put on by local musicians who are also regular customers. It was packed, and the energy level among attendees was high.

More notable and emotional for me is the way that they have embraced my mother-in-law, Karlyn, and her husband, Robert, as regular customers. Karlyn and Robert, both in their late eighties, are by no means your typical coffee house mavens. Like so many of the regulars at the Good Cup, they are not just customers; they are *known* there. The coffee shop hosted a birthday celebration for Robert's eighty-seventh birthday on a busy Saturday morning—and legend has it that Karlyn has her own key on the cash register, because she always gets a special order. On a more serious note, when Karlyn was diagnosed with breast cancer, the owners of the Good Cup brought a meal to her home. One of the fruits of empowerment is recognizing opportunities to show up in meaningful, memorable ways.

That is by no means "advertising," but it shows the power of connection. These interactions create a lot of positive energy. And here's the amazing news: this is where you, the small business owner, have a competitive edge. Starbucks isn't going to knock on someone's door and deliver them a home-cooked meal. But the small business owner, an integral part of the community? They will. That kind of connection is invaluable—not only for business but, even more importantly, for the community.

🧪 TO THE LAB!

I've included some resources to help you with your marketing in the "In Your Lab" resource section at the conclusion of chapter 6. See the Marketing Plan.

KEEP SOLICITING INPUT: THE FEEDBACK LOOP

Feedback is valuable fuel for your business. To maintain momentum, you want to keep the feedback loop going, with both customers, employees—and yourself. Checking in with yourself is one of the most important things you can do as an entrepreneur. That entrepreneurial energy you had at the start of this endeavor won't be consistent. It will see peaks and valleys. Asking yourself regularly if you've got the energy you need to continue, or if you need to tap into other energy sources like your team, is a good idea.

The same is true of your employees. You can't expect them to work like cogs in a machine. People will have their ups and downs. That's why I suggested having regular one-on-one meetings with your employees in chapter 4. Keep doing that. Remember that company I told you about that had such a culture crash they had to bring in a "mood elevator" to stabilize things? You don't want to end up there. Assessing your work environment regularly will help. In fact, at Pinnacle Bank (referenced in chapter 1 as a best-practice company on values-driven culture) the annual workplace environment survey results are consumed immediately by the CEO, with a multipage summary of his observations delivered to all leaders within days of receipt. He is all over it! You should be too.

With customers in particular, it's important to track reactions as you gain momentum. For example, if you add a new product or service, you want to know how they're received. Are you still moving in the right direction? Is an adjustment needed? Check in with the people you serve to make sure. You don't want to be caught by surprise if something you're doing isn't working—find out *before* you see an impact on your earnings.

Every great company has that bond with clients, that continual feedback loop. They want to know what people need, and they're constantly innovating toward that end. By consistently respecting that feedback loop over time, they can give their target market exactly what they're looking for. Trader Joe's is a fantastic example. The company doesn't just track sales and trends when deciding what to stock; they actually ask customers. For example, when a customer tried a soy ice cream cookie at a Southern California Trader Joe's, they subsequently requested it at their local Nevada store. Soon enough, the food market had stocked that soy ice cream cookie not only at that customer's store location but also at other locations.[25]

🧪 TO THE LAB!

I've included some resources to help you collect feedback at the conclusion of chapter 6. See the Energy Health Check (your personal feedback loop), Workplace Environment Survey (your employee feedback loop), and Client Satisfaction Survey (your customer feedback loop).

REMAIN READY FOR CHANGE: PROACTIVE RESILIENCE BUILDING

Maintaining momentum requires resilience. A lot of business owners get caught up in ideas of accelerating, growing, and *more, more, more*. It's just as important, if not more so, to make sure your business is strong and capable of withstanding whatever forces may be enacted on it. Do you have the stability that comes from resilience? Revisit all those forces we talked about in chapter 3—is your business equipped to handle them? What if there's a recession? What if there's a supply chain interruption? What if we have another pandemic on our hands? There

---

25   Jena McGregor, "Leading Listener: Trader Joe's," Fast Company, October 1, 2004, https://www.fastcompany.com/51637/leading-listener-trader-joes.

are a lot of things to think about. You can't anticipate every force, but resilience will help you bounce back when one hits your business hard.

How do you build resilience? A lot of it comes from your culture—now we're going way back to the mission and vision you articulated in chapter 1. Giving your company purpose and then coalescing people around that purpose (mass!) will make your business more resilient. Agility—the key to managing inertia—is another piece of resilience. Are agility, problem-solving, and innovation among your core values? Getting your stakeholders' support likewise builds resilience. Finally, you need some financial flexibility to be resilient. Helping small business owners achieve financial resilience is one of my areas of expertise, thanks to my career in banking, and it's something I'll talk about in detail in the next chapters.

There's this misconception that the biggest companies or the longest-standing ones are the most resilient, but that isn't always the case. Small business owners have a great advantage precisely because they are smaller, which makes it easier to control things like agility, inertia, and velocity. Older companies often have established processes that they get stuck in; they're too monolithic and set in their ways to have the flexibility that resilience demands. The world of "this is how we have always done it" is brittle and subject to shattering completely when confronted with unexpected adversity. This is where you, the entrepreneur, have the edge.

🧪 TO THE LAB!

I've included some resources to help you assess your resilience in the "In Your Lab" resource section at the conclusion of chapter 6. See the Multi-Vector Analysis and the Resilience Check.

Trust in What You've Built Enough to Grow

If you take care of all the pieces above and give consistent attention to your momentum, you should be able to trust in what you've built—enough so that you can grow, adding mass as you move and stoking the fuel box to maintain energy. Hopefully you have added mass already through intentional client acquisition with your USP. Sometimes, it seems that the market opportunity calls for something more. That could mean expanding into a new geographical market, for example, or adding a new product or service to your lineup.

I mentioned in the introduction that my dad worked in textiles. He worked for companies like Carter's and Hanes, and then he had an opportunity to join Nike. This was way back in 1980. At that point, Nike was only a footwear company and didn't sell apparel at any meaningful level (mostly promotionally), so my dad was part of the apparel initiative when he joined.

Today, Nike being *just* shoes is pretty unthinkable; in retrospect, adding apparel seems like such an obvious growth strategy. But by 1980 Nike had already grown to approximately $270 million in footwear sales, with no defined apparel effort. In 1980 Nike did $8 million in apparel sales; the next year, it was $33 million. By 2015, Nike was recognized as the most valuable apparel brand in the *world*, beating out luxury bigwigs like Louis Vuitton and Hermès.[26, 27] My kids can't imagine a world without Nike athletic apparel. Timing is always important, but sometimes we do not see the opportunities right at our fingertips. When we do see the chance to water a seed

26   "Annual Report," NIKE Inc., 1982, https://s1.q4cdn.com/806093406/files/doc_finan-cials/1982/1982%20annual%20report.pdf.

27   Vanessa Friedman, "Nike Is the Most Valuable Apparel Brand in the World," *New York Times*, May 29, 2015, https://www.nytimes.com/2015/05/30/fashion/nike-is-the-most-valuable-apparel-brand-in-the-world.html.

and grow, amazing things can spring forth; growth is energizing to anyone involved in it.

I also love the local example of LBMC, founded in Nashville as a traditional accounting firm by four partners with Big Eight firm experience in 1984. Slowly, the firm began testing offerings in related services such as payroll and other outsourceable HR functions. LBMC now offers IT, information security, and wealth advisory services, in addition to traditional accounting and HR. It is ranked in the top forty firms in the country—and it's a nationally certified Great Place to Work, whose seven-hundred-plus employees are "loving what they do and who they do it for."[28] In a video clip on LBMC's website, company founder David Morgan states, "We never wanted to be the biggest. We wanted to be the best." He goes on to stress the importance of continuous learning as a core company value. I do not know if the essence of mass building can be put more simply than that. It's no coincidence that this firm has sustained momentum for over forty years.

Some businesses fall into the trap of assuming the fastest and easiest way to grow will be through acquiring another company. This can be tricky, especially for smaller businesses where a major investment means more risk relative to their capitalization.

The motivations for acquisition are usually good. Maybe you're trying to get into a new market, or there's a new product you want to offer. However, you want to be very cautious about growing through acquisition. A lot of components need to be maintained for acquisitions to work, from company culture to finances. If they are not treated with caution, acquisitions threaten to be dilutive, reducing the mass of your company. Acquisitions also require a lot of energy. This

---

28 "About Us," LBMC, n.d., accessed September 25, 2023, https://www.lbmc.com/about-us/.

means you have less of that entrepreneurial energy to give to other areas, like your team or your customers.

Like any purchase, acquisitions can get emotional, and their success often depends on the best possible economics for the acquirer. It may seem like a luxury and an expense you cannot afford on the front end, but hiring a business valuation expert typically pays for itself many times over because you are optimizing the economics of the deal.

Now, I'm not saying acquisition is always a poor choice. My only point is that there are many other ways you can grow, and it's worth exploring those options. Growth can be a big part of momentum, what any small business aspires to. Just make sure you aren't sacrificing your attention to the other points I've mentioned to pursue acquisition-based growth solely. Momentum requires consistent and careful attention to the entire freight train, from the engine to the brakes; otherwise you risk a breakdown—or going off the rails completely.

The Dangers of Friction in Slowing Momentum

Maintaining momentum is largely about maintaining energy. It requires consistency over time to keep your business going in the direction you want it to go in, at the level and speed you desire. You'll find yourself coming back to the things you dealt with at the very start of your business journey, from your business plan to your SWOT analysis. I hope that isn't discouraging to you. I just want to be realistic about the work involved. Just like any job, you must keep showing up if you want your small business to thrive.

In this chapter, I've outlined some of the areas that will require your continual attention if you want your momentum to continue and grow. These are proactive steps you can take to keep that train chugging along the tracks. They will help you maintain your momentum, especially if you are consistent over time.

But there are also things that can get in the way of your momentum and slow it down—points of friction that can arise unexpectedly, requiring a reactive response. While you can't always foresee these points of friction, there are some common ones you can possibly anticipate and prepare for. If you learn how to use friction to your advantage, it can even *help* your business gain traction and maintain momentum. The next chapter explains how it's done.

🧪 IN YOUR LAB

At the beginning of this chapter, I asked what actions you're taking to ensure momentum toward your business's goals. How can you identify and eliminate the forces that might slow you down? These resources from the Bizzics website can help:

- **Business Plan:** This document should be revised every three years, at least. Is it time to revisit yours?

- **SWOT Analysis:** You likely did a SWOT analysis when you were just getting your business off the ground. Repeated analyses help ensure you're still on track!

- **Competitive Advantage Plan:** Is that USP you defined at the start of your business journey still relevant? Let's find out.

- **Competitor Analysis:** Again, you probably did a competitor analysis when you were just founding your business. This is also something you should review regularly. Is yours up to date?

- **Marketing Plan:** A marketing plan helps your business maintain momentum, reminding existing customers you exist and attracting new ones.

- **Energy Health Check:** Check in with yourself. How is your entrepreneurial energy doing since you began your journey? Is it still high, or is it lagging?

- **Workplace Environment Survey:** Make sure your team is still happy as your business changes and grows. Keep an eye out for possible areas for improvement.

- **Client Satisfaction Survey:** Keep getting feedback from customers, again and again.

- **Multi-Vector Analysis:** The vectors that impact your business will change with time. Let's check in and see where they're at now.

- **Resilience Health Check:** Make sure you're building a resilient business that can maintain momentum and stand the test of time.

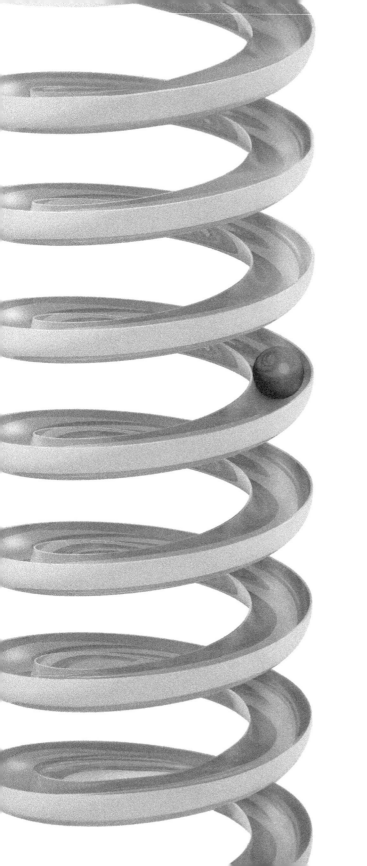

Friction

Friction is present in virtually every circumstance, yet we don't really appreciate its usefulness until we no longer have it. Have you ever walked down your driveway or front walk after a snowstorm or ice storm—and had your feet slip right out from under you? A lack of friction can be dangerous. But too much friction can also be a risk. Perhaps you were once cavalier about changing your car's oil and saw smoke coming out from under your hood—or smelled that sickening scent of metal on metal. While we tend to associate it with danger, friction is actually one of our greatest friends in moving forward, in life or in business.

I probably think about friction more often than most people. Nashville is home to the headquarters of Bridgestone Americas, Inc. The tire conglomerate has the naming rights to our primary indoor arena, home to the NHL's Nashville Predators. They also have a beautiful downtown skyscraper, with a rooftop that's designed to resemble a tire tread—an innovative way to hide the typical industrial equipment that serves the building while also reminding the public that Bridgestone is all about safe travels.

Bridgestone has a tread design for just about anything. The idea is that you want the right level of friction for the surfaces you will encounter on your journey, whether that takes you across snow, gravel, dirt, rain, ice—you name it.

Growing up in North Carolina, I have been exposed to stock car racing for decades. If you're into racing, you may know that NASCAR's origins are in running moonshine on backcountry roads during the Prohibition era. Today, NASCAR's races aren't held on dirt roads but on short tracks, long tracks, and superspeedways—with the average speed varying nearly one hundred miles per hour between the short track and the superspeedway. A NASCAR race car's tires must be designed to negotiate four left turns per lap. Imagine how those tread designs are engineered to factor in vehicle weight, speed, and the surface on which the car is racing.

Just north of Nashville is the Music City Raceway, the oldest International Hot Rod Association (IHRA) track in the country. Here, the cars run straight ahead for one-eighth of a mile. The tires used in those cases are generally called "racing slicks" and have no tread at all. They're built for speed.

Friction is created when two imperfect surfaces—not completely smooth—meet each other. There is some unevenness that creates a bite between the surfaces, which allows for movement but also creates heat as the two surfaces interact. Sometimes, as in primitive fire building, we want the heat. Other times, as with tires, we put up with the heat because we want the movement. The most common cause of tire blowouts on roadways is overinflation and underinflation, either of which can lead to excess friction: even with the perfect tread design for the conditions, too much or too little pressure will affect friction in a way that literally makes a tire explode.

So, what does friction look like in business? I've seen business owners grapple with two main types of friction: friction among people and financial friction. While energy is created from the friction present in businesses, what every business owner really wants is to move forward, adhering to the business plans established in regular planning cycles. That is the road that you are on, and you get to decide the appropriate level of friction to achieve what you set out to do—that level where things are so in control that no one ever talks about friction. They just enjoy the benefits of it.

Unfortunately, business owners don't have a stated "recommended pressure" they can refer to—like on the side of a tire—when figuring out how much friction is right for their business. Every entrepreneur must decide for themselves how much air to put in the tires and thereby how much friction to create. It is a highly intuitive decision based on your knowledge of your people as well as market challenges and opportunities.

Let's consider the implications of people friction and financial friction within your business—and look at how to navigate both so that you can safely keep your car on the track.

🔑 KEY BUSINESS QUESTION:

Where are the sources of friction in your business—energetically and financially? What is causing friction in your leadership style, making it harder to address the energetic and financial points?

People Friction

Once you have set your perfect business plan in place, your objective is to achieve it. Hopefully your goals are clearly aligned—growth goals, client satisfaction goals, and profitability goals. To me, these goals are more than an objective. They are a covenant among employees, customers, and company owners that ensure that the promise of the business's vision and mission is realized and, over time, maximized.

The challenge is that what you *need* people to do and what they *want* to do or feel comfortable doing may not be a smooth, natural match. That friction should be healthy and energy creating. As the business owner, your job is to survey the landscape for opportunities and then match those opportunities with the team you have. Create these matches with goals in mind that not only align with your business's long-term success and distinguish you as a top performer among peers, but also stretch your employees' creativity and personal growth enough to generate some energy. Most of us have heard the SMART acronym dictating that goals should be specific, measurable, achievable, relevant, and timebound. It is simple and true.

Yet small business owners experience challenges in setting and communicating goals. I have seen the drive for a close-knit "family" environment take precedence over setting challenging goals. It is a frictionless environment that almost guarantees you'll come up short. I have also seen business owners struggle in communicating goals. Financial goals in particular can be shrouded in darkness when business owners are overly guarded about sharing too much information about the company, especially as it relates to profits. Finally, I have seen goals limited to the sales force and top-line revenue growth, when the reality is that every single person in your company needs a goal to make your plan a reality.

Once your plan is set, every person needs a set of individual goals that contributes to achieving the plan. The best organizations I have witnessed have target goals as well as stretch goals that include greater rewards for employees. In my experience, stretch goals, if clearly communicated and incentivized, are usually adopted as the true objectives. I love *The 4 Disciplines of Execution: Achieving Your Wildly Important Goals*, by Chris McChesney, Jim Huling, and Sean Covey; the book stresses the importance of goals beyond achieving a desired end result.

Unlike the annual planning session, holding people accountable to goals is much more time sensitive because the clock is running on your year. Monthly accountability sessions are a minimum standard for me. In this age of data availability and collection, I have seen very healthy environments in companies that have weekly and even daily accountability check-ins. It really depends on the nature of your business.

That accountability process will highlight hot spots of what you need versus what people are able to do or willing to do. Sometimes clarity and repetition of objectives will help people rise to the occasion. Sometimes you may discover that the employee is incapable of producing the results required. Somewhere in between are coaching opportunities for growth. Only you know your aptitude and capacity for that. Maybe it is a growth frontier for you personally to learn how to coach effectively—I don't know. What I *do* know is that nonperforming employees quickly produce unhealthy friction in a company and that their nonperformance virtually guarantees you'll take an undesired detour from your plan.

One final topic on goal achievement I would like to address is the highly seasonal business and the level of friction required to persevere through make-or-break seasons. For a couple of summers in college, I worked in the Nike warehouse in Memphis, unloading tractor-trailers of Nike footwear. To this day, I believe it is the most difficult job I have ever had—not the worst, but the most difficult. I was at the tail end of Nike fulfilling its annual sales plan, a vast majority of which came during back-to-school season.

Memphis in mid-July is about as hot and humid as it gets. We would arrive in the very early morning hours to literally dozens of forty-foot trailers full of product that had to be unloaded and shelved, to then be picked and shipped. I will never forget that our "lead man" was named Earl Early. He was ex-military and a driver. By July, we had our system down. We attacked each trailer with a vengeance, digging deeper and deeper into the heat-baked nose of the trailer, throwing and stacking boxes by product type and size, sweeping it out before moving on to the next one. I remember quickly learning that a case of football cleats weighs a lot more than running shoes! Earl would be barking in the background, celebrating as we went along, but never relenting. I would go home covered in cardboard dust, having inhaled more than was probably healthy.

Earl knew from his military experience how to create a high level of friction to produce results. By early to mid-August, the game had been played, and Earl was more likely to jawbone around with us before many of us seasonal employees departed to school. We knew what we signed up for, and we knew what Earl was being asked to achieve for the company. While we had occasional spats between employees, there was a certain respect for Earl, who was making sure we got the job done.

There are times when conditions change, and a higher level of friction is required to navigate the road ahead. In seasonal businesses, it is absolutely necessary, or else you will get off plan altogether. Do not be afraid to escalate when your plan requires it. I believe that employees enjoy celebrating a peak performance. The key is keeping it in the context of the broader vision.

Now, let's acknowledge the likelihood of unhealthy friction *among* your employees: different personalities, interdependencies among employees and job functions, that all-too-human urge to point the crooked finger of blame. My deeply held personal belief is that you must have an environment in which there is a willingness to *create* friction when the plan is at risk.

I have seen plenty of companies choose problem-solving, partnership, and collaboration as core values. I admire that. I also think it is naive and shortsighted to believe it is always going to happen that way. We are human beings, after all, each of us with our own triggers and sensitivities, and things just boil over. Despite a generally synchronized work group on the Nike freight docks, I also remember a full case of shoes being thrown at my head one particularly hot summer day. If the conveyor line had not been between me and the thrower, old Joe College here probably would have been pulverized.

The key in these instances is recovery and moving forward. Conflict resolution skills should be a key competency for your company. Things can get out of hand very quickly. As explained in chapter 4, "Mass," so much is at risk in the bonds between you and your employees, and among your employees. The best book I have ever read on conflict resolution is *Crucial Conversations: Tools for*

Talking When Stakes Are High, by Kerry Patterson, Joseph Grenny, Ron McMillan, and Al Switzler. You may have others you like. Just make sure you are doing something to maintain an *appropriate* level of friction to achieve the plan that you designed for your business. All your employees will benefit from it, both at work and outside of work.

A lot of these soft skills link to the leader's roles and responsibilities discussed in chapter 5: it's your job to inspire, motivate, empower, communicate, and maintain consistency. These behaviors will also help you manage the appropriate level of friction and keep moving forward without letting things get out of control (or worse, toxic).

Remember, all these skills can be learned. You do not need to pay tens of thousands for an Ivy League MBA to acquire leadership acumen. Great leaders are truly made, not born. I mentioned early in the book that even small business owners can benefit from leadership training, and it's a belief I feel necessary to repeat—because I've seen poor leadership derail many a small business. And I've seen great leadership take businesses to amazing places.

Financial Friction

Liquidity is everything in business. As long as you have cash, you can keep going. When I discussed friction with my friend Marcus, he made an observation that had my jaw on the floor: he noted that some vessels are so massive that they literally cannot be transported across land—but when they sit in water, they can be easily moved with an engine that has a fraction of the power needed to move large loads across land. The smooth liquid surface of the water allows for nearly frictionless movement. Great liquidity makes things nearly frictionless in business as well.

Some small percentage of companies are fortunate to have significant capital raises that end up in what we call a *burn rate*. Cash is being burned, but the company isn't necessarily profitable, or cash isn't flowing on an operational basis. Their day will come! For most companies, liquidity starts with cash flow and ends with how much you are able to retain.

The term *cash flow* is often a catch-all phrase used vaguely in loan requests. What it means to me is that the company no longer has sufficient cash to sustain operations. Now as much as I dread the idea of a workplace with toxic levels of friction, this kind of financial friction is even more deadly. Forget the tires; this is like having no oil left in your engine. Everything grinds to a stop, and the engine gets so badly damaged that it may never recover.

From my experience, cash flow is usually a profitability problem. Part of your rolling three-year plan is an operating budget. That budget includes both revenues and expenses. Simply put, your profit is the difference between the two. When that gap closes and your expenses are butted right up against your revenue, or exceeding revenue and creating losses, you have financial friction. As long as you have cash (liquidity) to bridge the gap, you can make it. Otherwise, you're sunk.

I have seen thousands of business plans over the years, and very few that portray operating losses. Those are the ones most likely to have a capital raise and burn rate. By and large, business plans are built based on averages and assumptions that may or may not be the reality. In his timeless leadership text, *Leadership Is An Art*, Max De Pree suggests that the first responsibility of any leader is to define reality. Your operating budget is a great place to start giving yourself a reality check.

MANAGING THE MARGIN

The gross margin is the lifeblood of any business. It is the gap between the price of a product or service and the variable cost of producing or rendering it. From that margin, the remainder of all other costs are covered. Whatever is left is your profit. When budgets are put together, there must be a certain level of precision in understanding what it costs to produce your product or deliver your service. Even more importantly, you need precision and confidence in establishing your price, or what your product or service is worth to your target customer. Now, we are circling back to your USP and your competitor analysis! It seems so basic, but there are so many facets in the psychology of a business owner that can distort reality.

> ## 🧪 TO THE LAB!
>
> I've included some resources to help you with your profit margin management in the "In Your Lab" resource section at the conclusion of chapter 7. See the Profit Health Check and Profit Increase Calculator.

PRICING

Here are some things that can be happening to you on pricing. First, you underprice out of fear that you will not meet your sales plan, or you launch with promotional prices that become permanent. Second, you overestimate the differentiation in your product because you, personally, are crazy about the product. Finally, you underestimate the competitive response of established competitors, not only in pricing but also in how quickly they respond to a newly differentiated offering.

Product pricing embodies the value of what you have brought to the market. It is the place with the most intense psychology around how strongly you believe in yourself and what your target clients expect and value. Pricing should be the most sober and analytical yet affirming aspect of your business, brimming with that quiet confidence that *we are worth it*—and never backing down. Many years ago, I had a banking executive tell me, "Price is only an issue in the absence of value." I have never forgotten that. If you are like me, you would much rather spend time thinking about how to become more valuable than depreciating yourself and all your employees through discounting. Go back to your bonds with your clients and how well you understand what is most important to them.

> ## ⚗ TO THE LAB!
>
> I've included some resources to help you with your pricing strategy at the conclusion of chapter 7. See the Pricing Strategy Infographic.

VARIABLE COSTS

The other side of establishing appropriate friction in your gross margin is the variable cost to produce or deliver. It is not that hard to find industry averages for margins, but anyone with even a basic understanding of statistics knows how misleading an average is. This is your unique offering in your specific market—what does it cost *you* to produce or deliver it? How many possible suppliers do you have, and what is their history of pricing and consistent supply? The COVID-19 pandemic made this extremely difficult to assess over the past few years, but it is work that needs to be done proactively and consistently for you to maintain appropriate friction in gross margin.

Gross margin drives the ultimate survival of your business and even the ultimate *value* of your business. For many investors and acquirers, it is the first line of your financials that they assess. Stay in touch with your clients. Stay in touch with your suppliers. Understand their sensitivities and have a plan for all likely scenarios. Some of the most successful small business owners I know do not react; they *act,* passing on small price increases quarterly that protect their margin and do not shock or upset their customers.

FIXED COSTS

Your business has many expenses that are simply the cost of doing business, whether occupancy, salaried employees, marketing programs, or simple administrative needs. As much as we think we do, we never really know at the outset what expenses provide the highest level of efficiency and effectiveness in operations. It's an iterative process to understand what works best for you, what is most scalable, and what provides the absolute best support to the gross margin equation we discussed just a minute ago. In a way, it's another aspect of our mass discussion from chapter 4. Have you winnowed expenses down to the best of the best for maximum impact, or are unseen or unmanaged costs grinding away at your gross margin and creating unnecessary financial friction? We will hit this topic a bit more in the next chapter, "Leverage."

TRUST IN YOUR OPERATING PLAN …

Your ability to manage financial friction is the difference between making it or not making it. It's the difference between a comfortable retirement and generational wealth—or prolonged work years. Wouldn't it be nice if there were a magic solution to make sure you get it right? Look to your operating plan. Your operating plan is your road map to sustainability when it comes to finances.

What's more, there is always a way to make your plan work. I love that scene in the movie *Apollo 13* where the team on the ground is trying to figure out how to help the astronauts up in space with a spaceship malfunction, a leaking oxygen tank and a lack of fuel cells. The problem is, the spaceship crew can only use items they already have on board to make repairs. So, one of the big bosses at NASA throws a bunch of junk on the table in the middle of all these brilliant engineers—plastic tubing, rubber gloves, I don't know what else—and tells them to figure it out. That's what they've got to work with.

In the end, they come up with a plan using those rudimentary goods. One skeptic goes dark and says that the incident could become the greatest disaster NASA has ever experienced. Another retorts, "With all due respect, sir, this will be NASA's finest hour."[29] Anybody who knows me knows that I quote this line all the time—often when it looks like I'm about to get into trouble! And I think that attitude can take you far in business. You can achieve a lot with some creativity.

BUT DON'T BE AFRAID TO ASK FOR HELP!

Finances can be intimidating to a lot of business owners. Unfortunately, worries about dealing with the intricacies of details like profit margins, cash flow, and more keep some of them from getting into the details of their financials. It's not until that high-heat moment of financial friction—depleted cash reserves, bills to pay, payroll to make, debts to service—that alarm bells go off.

Just as banking for small businesses has trended toward online, self-service models over the past couple of decades, we've similarly seen the rise of accounting software such as Quicken and Quick-Books. While such technology is helpful and beneficial, it doesn't offer personalized, practice-based *strategic* advice on things like pricing decisions, production costs, and budgeting practices. Many small business owners hire bookkeepers with software expertise to keep costs

---

29 *Apollo 13*, directed by Ron Howard (Universal Pictures, Imagine Entertainment, and RLJE Films, 1995), https://www.imdb.com/title/tt0112384/.

down. My encouragement to you is to get the *professional advice* that you deserve from professionals. The heat shield was everything when Apollo 13 reentered the earth's atmosphere. Professional financial advice is your heat shield for financial friction. If you want to start learning, one of the best books on business profitability that I know is *Profit First: Transform Your Business from a Cash-Eating Monster to a Money-Making Machine*, by Mike Michalowicz.

STAYING LIQUID

Let's get back to the idea of liquidity, a nearly frictionless environment in which barges and ships can be moved with surprisingly little motive power. It is the cushion you need to absorb short-term cost spikes, slow-paying customers, and unexpected outlays—all things that fall outside your plan.

We started with profitability because your profits feed your balance sheet. All the earnings you accumulate end up invested in assets of some kind: receivables, inventory, fixed assets, and, of course, *cash*! The earnings you retain end up in the equity section of your balance sheet, which is the longest-term funding source available to you. The difference between your total assets and your equity is various forms of debt—short-term obligations like accounts payable and short-term lines of credit borrowings and long-term financing such as term loans. Accounting principles require balance.

I do not want to ignore the importance of managing tax liability legally and appropriately. Every dollar you pay in taxes is one fewer dollar going to this important part of your balance sheet. This is another point where paying for professional experience is worth every penny. Bad tax decisions can burden you for years.

While total cash on hand is the purest form of liquidity, another measurement is something called working capital, which is the gap between short-term assets and short-term obligations. You can imagine, and may have experienced, the friction when the short-term bills you must pay are equal to or greater than your short-term assets. You're constantly trying to collect to cover your obligations. Again, it's like the metal pieces in your car engine gnashing together with no oil. The result? Too much heat!

When you produce ample profit and retain that profit in your business, you are effectively replacing short-term obligations with long-term funding and creating that space, working capital, that enables you to float through the unexpected or temporary. The thing to remember is that lots of bad things happen to boats when the water level is low, exposing all kinds of hazards that ground the vessel or destroy it altogether. Your business is the same with respect to liquidity. Bills must be paid.

Even when you have run your profit plan to perfection and retained those profits in your business, your cash position can be compromised by simply not managing assets well. I see this mostly in managing billings and collections, either not billing immediately at the time the product is shipped or service delivered, or allowing clients to string you along, extending their terms, which makes your cash position poor, even though your working capital position may be strong. In addition, be very cautious about paying cash for fixed assets unless your working capital is exceptionally strong. You may need that cash in a pinch.

I had a wonderful professor in my MBA program at Kenan-Flagler Business School, Dick Levin, who wrote one of the most beautifully simple business books: *Buy Low, Sell High, Collect Early, Pay Late: The Manager's Guide to Financial Survival*. It is truly the secret sauce to relieving financial friction and produces almost miraculous results when managed consistently. I knew a company here in Nashville that arranged fifteen-day terms from customers and forty-five-day terms from suppliers, creating thirty days of interest-free financing in its trade cycle. More typically, companies collect cash deposits on sales. Now, don't forget: you still need profit in the sale, or it will catch up with you in the long run. Profit comes first.

Financial friction is avoidable if managed well, but like so many parts of your business, it is not one thing, it is many things—things that connect your income statement to your balance sheet and ultimately determine how high the heat is on your cash flow. Your goal is to avoid too much heat-generating financial friction. The solution? Stay liquid!

🧪 TO THE LAB!

I've included some resources to help you with your cash flow in the "In Your Lab" resource section at the conclusion of chapter 7. See the Understanding Cash Cycles Infographic, Cash Flow Forecast Template, and Creating a Cash Reserve Checklist.

Leadership: Your Key to Managing Friction– and Capitalizing on Leverage

Friction, whether energetic or financial, doesn't have to be a bad thing. It can be the friend you need to help your business maintain deliberate momentum. It's the treads on your business-vehicle's tires, helping you ease around curves and conquer snowy roads safely. Friction can be very necessary in the business world—I've seen its value firsthand through my experience in the banking industry.

In banking, there is constant friction between the people that are producing loan opportunities and the people that are underwriting them. When it comes to potentially issuing credit, there are many dynamics to consider, from the broader economic climate to industry-specific changes. For the bank, the lender, the sole interest is not to absorb losses. That said, there are individuals in the industry who are out there trying to build relationships with people and build up a loan portfolio for the bank. They are at the complete other end of the spectrum in their orientation to the bank. They get paid for different things.

I've seen different levels of friction between those two groups. Sometimes it works, and everybody is moving in a direction that's healthy for the bank. Other times, it doesn't work. For example, if there isn't enough friction in the system on the loan production side, then you get piles of bad loans. On the other hand, if the loan portfolio isn't growing, there's no revenue growth. A healthy amount of friction helps keep the balance.

However, friction, whether energetic or financial, can be destructive too. That's when good leaders must step up. One problem with friction is that it's so embedded in all we do we don't always notice it at first. Think of starting a fire with two sticks—something I watched my son learn as a Scout. At first, the sticks rub together and create just a little bit of energy and heat. But then they can create a spark—and, in the end, an entire blaze.

As a business owner, you've got to catch the signs of friction before you've got a wildfire on your hands. Too often, entrepreneurs don't notice friction until it's become a serious problem—the employees are walking out, or the cash flow is negative, or the coffers are empty. If you're trying to figure out friction at *that* point, you've got a lot of work ahead.

Good leaders catch the friction early. That's a big part of what great leaders do: they constantly evaluate friction points and try to make it easy to do business. That could mean everything from making it easy for employees to do their jobs to making it easy for customers to complete a transaction. It means reviewing your financial data regularly, with an eye for details like profit margins and cash flow.

Basically, managing friction in your business means you've got to keep checking the tires of the car. Give the tires a kick. Is there enough air in them? Check the treads. Are they worn down? Does a tire need replacing? Scope out the weather. Is there a change coming that means it's time to swap out your regular tires for your winter tires? We've talked about a few possible friction points in this chapter, so now they should be on your radar. When you're checking the tires of your car, you'll know what to look for.

Managing friction in your business is part of your responsibility as a leader of that business. And even if your business is small, just you and a couple of workers, you've still got to lead! You are the one in charge—of yourself, your business, and your employees.

Great leadership will help you manage friction in your business. It's also what will allow you to tap into the powerful levers you and your business possess—levers that can springboard your company to greater heights. Leverage in business can make a big difference in your success, and that's what we'll discuss in the final chapter.

🧪 IN YOUR LAB

At the beginning of this chapter, I asked you to consider the points of friction in your business—from an energy, financial, and leadership standpoint. These resources can help as you navigate those friction points:

- **Profit Health Check:** Don't wait until your profits are less than you'd like. Examine your profit health *now*, before a nasty surprise arises.

- **Profit Increase Calculator:** Could you increase your profits? What would it take? Here's a tool to help you figure it out.

- **Choosing a Balanced Pricing Strategy Infographic:** A smart pricing strategy can help you maintain positive profit margins. Consult this infographic to get yours just right.

- **Understanding Cash Cycles Infographic:** An understanding of cash cycles can help you stay on top of cash flow. This infographic covers the basics.

- **Cash Flow Forecast Template:** What can you anticipate from your business's cash flow? Use this forecasting tool to get a better idea of what to expect.

- **Creating a Cash Reserve Checklist:** Do you have a cushion to fall back on if your cash flow falters? Use this tool to start building up this valuable resource.

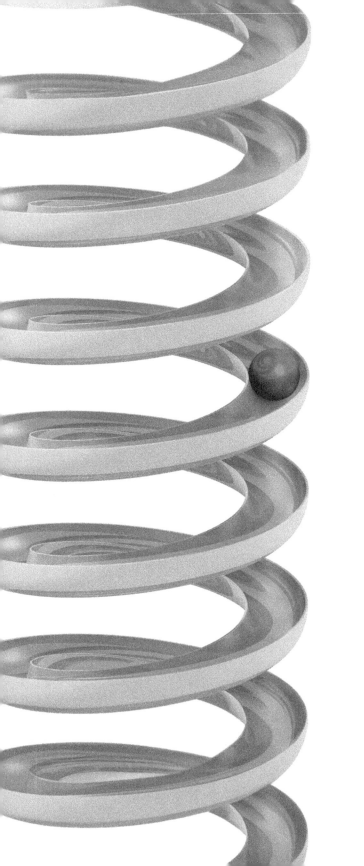

CHAPTER 8

Leverage

I marvel at the natural wonders of the world as much as the next guy. Mammoth Cave is not far from where I live. I will never forget climbing Black Elk Peak in South Dakota with one of my sons, and the Cliffs of Moher in western Ireland are truly breathtaking. Of course, the world is also full of man-made wonders—some of which seem like impossible feats. Do you have a favorite "how did they do that" place? Many people would claim the pyramids of Giza as that place. My personal favorite is the Newgrange portal tomb in Ireland.

Newgrange is some one thousand years older than the pyramids of Giza and perfectly designed to illuminate the inner chamber for approximately fifteen minutes on the winter solstice. The engineering feat of that alone is astounding. In both cases—Giza and New-grange—I wonder how they moved these massive boulders into place. Newgrange contains five different types of rock, none of it native to the area. I'm sure that our lesson on friction had a lot to do with it:

primitive barging on Ireland's many rivers may have provided the literal liquidity needed to transport such massive stones.

But what about moving those stones across land? I'm fairly certain that it had a lot to do with something called *leverage*. In theory, leverage enables you to cover distance more quickly than if you were relying on your power alone. The lever's fulcrum multiplies the power of the force applied.

My mind races with images of how those Stone Age farmers rallied to build their sacred place. Based on the size of the boulders I observed, it probably took more than one lever. I learned the hard way that it's not that easy to maximize leverage.

I'm an avid gardener, so I spend a good amount of time with a shovel in my hand, digging around in my yard. Tennessee is a rocky state, and I've broken more than one shovel in my backyard trying to dig up rocks to clear away the stony soil and make room for fresh, soft earth that will support a thriving garden. I'll be rooting around in the dirt, eager to get some giant boulder out—and the wooden handle will snap right off, usually right above the spade. If I used an iron pinch bar, that wouldn't happen—the bar would be strong enough to leverage the stone right out of the earth. But I'm usually using some old wooden-handled shovel—which breaks.

The same thing can happen to your business, including the people in it. You have certain levers in your business—human, organizational, and financial—that can serve as powerful tools. Just like a shovel, those levers can help get rid of the stones in your business garden, ensuring a thriving landscape for growth that sees your original business vision bear fruit. However, those levers must be strong enough to absorb the pressures they encounter.

There's a lot of talk in the business world about *leverage*. People say things like "Oh, I'm going to leverage my marketing capabilities," or "I'm going to leverage my people," or similar. When it comes to leveraging this or that, there are a lot of assumptions that whatever they're leveraging is strong enough to absorb the pressure that they're going to put on it. But it isn't always. If that lever is dried out and brittle, like my old wooden shovel handle, it might break. It might even break if it's new and untested—you never know.

In business, your levers can help you through moments of inertia or help you shift your direction when external vector forces come at your business. When those moments strike, where you're stuck or need to change course, you want to reach for your lever to help you remain agile. In business, those levers can be human, organizational, or financial. Let's talk about how you can check and leverage the strengths of all three.

🔑 KEY BUSINESS QUESTION:

What and who are the levers in your business?

Human

Your strongest lever of all comes back to your mass—the people you've packed your business with, and how densely packed and well connected they are. Remember, the human component starts with you and your entrepreneurial energy, which you want to keep high. However, it extends well beyond you, to your employees and, of course, your customers. Think of the examples of densely packed businesses I've given—like the Good Cup, the coffee shop in Nashville that celebrated twenty years in the business with all its regular customers attending.

That little business has stood the test of time, surviving the surge of giants like Starbucks and more. I believe it's in part thanks to the strength of this most important lever, the people within the business and surrounding it. When humanity coalesces around a common source, there is nothing more powerful. Even if the shovel breaks, there are people on hand to tape it back together.

How can you make sure your human lever is strong? Well, check in with the humans who compose it, of course! That means checking in with yourself and assessing your own energy and motivation, as well as checking in with your employees and considering their satisfaction. Finally, you've got to keep the lines of communication open with your customers. Someone once told me that the first big test of a leader is making the "big ask." Only then will you know how solid you are.

> ## 🧪 TO THE LAB!
>
> I've included some resources to help you assess your people levers in the "In Your Lab" resource section at the conclusion of chapter 8. See the Energy Health Check, Workplace Environment Survey, and Client Satisfaction Survey.

Organizational

Your organizational levers are multifaceted. They include your values, vision, and mission—as well as your USP, the value-add you give your customers. A lot of your organizational levers are found in your business's key competencies, notably the elements that might appear in your SWOT analysis.

I think of Apple's competency for creative, intuitive design that created raving fans of PC users and catapulted it to a dominant position in digital music. I think of Jeff Bezos's genius for distribution, incubated in his garage and grown exponentially through his workforce of innovators—from books to music to movies and more. I think of the number of banks in the US shrinking by 75 percent in my forty-year career, and how many of the survivors have been experts at mergers and integrations. I think of Pinnacle Bank and the discipline they have for hiring the best people and retaining them through a masterful workplace environment.

All those examples may sound way out of reach for small business owners. Yet the reality is that all those businesses started with just a handful of people who knew that they would need strong levers to grow to their potential. And, for all the franchise owners out there or aspiring franchisors, you might consider franchising a defined operating system to be leveraged. Implemented correctly, this lever can move an aspiring entrepreneur to their goals more quickly.

Just like you want to keep checking on the humans who make up your business success, you also want to keep checking on the core competencies that make up your business success. That could include your USP, your processes, your marketing, and more. It requires identifying where you're performing well and pinpointing where there's room for improvement—and then, of course, fixing it if necessary.

That usually means asking some challenging questions. The USP that was once truly unique and valuable may no longer be as valuable if the competition is catching up to you. How can you be sure that your strengths are still your strengths? Rerunning your SWOT analysis at regular intervals is one way to be certain.

⚗ TO THE LAB!

I've included some resources to help you assess your organizational levers in the "In Your Lab" resource section at the conclusion of chapter 8. See the SWOT Analysis.

Financial

Finally, there's financial leverage, usually talked about in terms of a company's balance sheet but with operating implications as well. In many ways, financial leverage is more obvious than leveraging people and systems. Basic things like home ownership are expedited by debt. You leverage your 20 percent down payment with 80 percent debt, and you have a piece of the rock! Anyone could save to pay cash over time, but most desire ownership faster. Businesses are no different and require strict discipline regarding equity and debt to survive.

Throughout your business journey, whether at the start or later on, you will likely seek funding. In business, people talk about "leveraging the company up." Most business owners hit a point where they start to think about taking on more debt in the company, for one reason or another. This isn't necessarily a bad thing. If you could borrow more money, maybe you could fund a new location or hire more people or invest in more marketing—whatever your motivation may be. That debt that you take on enables you to move the company faster than you could if you saved up and tried to retain your earnings for ten to fifteen years. Debt *can* become a lever!

However, it's important to understand that not all funding sources have the same qualities. There are multiple varieties of financing, each with their own "tensile strength." Being financially overleveraged is dangerous and can result in bankruptcy. Ultimately, the question always becomes how much equity you have in the company, either through what you put in at the beginning, through other investors, or through money that you've retained from earnings over time.

The money that you've put in and retained, you have 100 percent say over. That portion of your capitalization will be rock solid. There's no claim on it; it's your money. Nothing bad can happen with that part of it. You get to decide if you want to take the money back out or not.

With debt, it's different—each type of debt will place different obligations on you. Money is a commodity that takes on the characteristics of its owners. Some are patient; some are not. Some are particularly greedy. Some are control freaks. Pay attention to the motives and "personalities" of your funding sources.

Here is a good example. Banks are very conservative by nature because the money they lend is not theirs. It belongs to their depositors. So, they are more focused than others on getting their money back quickly. If you initiate a line of credit to fund asset growth, it is likely to have a one-year maturity, which means you will be back at the bank, trying to get that loan renewed, and the money itself could disappear.

On the other hand, you could initiate a permanent working capital loan for growth purposes through the SBA and obtain a seven- or ten-year term. This is much more durable and offers more "tensile strength" as you move your company forward. Many people balk at the paperwork involved in SBA lending, but in my view, it is one of the strongest levers a small business could hope for, besides equity.

Small business funding is a crazy landscape today. Like so many things that have evolved over time, there are more options than ever—including credit card financing, "hard money" lenders, angel investors, accounts receivable financing, manufacturer financing, and banks of all shapes and sizes with specific industry interests and aversions. My caution to you is that money may all *look* the same, but it is *not* the same. And if you are building a lever to move your company to great heights, you need to understand the characteristics of the money you secure.

In business financial analysis, leverage is the ratio of total debt to equity. Many companies operate quite well at ratios of three to one and lower. The higher the ratio, the less margin for error you have. You don't want to have so much debt to service that you default if just one client doesn't pay you on time—or you're unable to absorb typical seasonal cycles of losses and profits. I have seen companies leveraged at ten to one or more; they effectively keep borrowing through online lenders and "hard money" sources just to keep their debts current.

Depending on how you leverage up the equity in your company, you could have a tool that is completely fragile and prone to break at the next big rock—or a very sustainable, handy tool, a lever that helps you move ahead faster than you could have otherwise. If you want to keep moving your company forward, you'll likely have to keep taking on debt, and you'll have to be very deliberate and disciplined in how much and what type of debt you take on.

For those interested in growing by acquisition, please understand that the term *leveraged buyout* applies as much to you as it did to Michael Milken and the big corporate raiders of the 1980s and 1990s. Managing leverage is all about managing your margin for error. In an acquisition, there are so many unknowns—you should be very cautious about leveraging the acquisition to the hilt.

I have talked mostly about debt, but before we leave this important topic, let's talk about equity. There are also shiny new objects beyond the business itself that people may pursue. It's not uncommon for a hardworking entrepreneur to attain a certain level of business success and say, "I deserve a new home"—and to then take some of the capital out of the company to fund that new home. Now, I'm not saying that kind of reward isn't deserved! I just want to raise the red flag of caution. If you take $100,000 out of your business to buy a property (say, as a dividend) that immediately affects the ratio of how much debt to equity you have in your business—because you've shrunk your equity.

There's also operating leverage—which is basically the output that you get from your fixed costs. Most measure it in terms of how many cents of fixed costs it takes to produce one dollar of revenue. Small business owners are very aspirational on this front, determined to keep fixed costs down to the bare minimum. So, most companies improve this lever over time. As you move your company forward, you get smarter about where you spend your money, from marketing to people.

Over time, you're cutting wasted costs. So, while you might start with an operating leverage of 80 percent, later that might be whittled down to 50 percent. That's one way to make the lever stronger.

> ## 🧪 TO THE LAB!
>
> I've included some resources to help you assess your financial levers in the "In Your Lab" resource section at the conclusion of chapter 8. See the Financial Health Check and Financial Performance One-Pager.

Know Your Business; Know Your Levers

Understanding your business's levers is basically a question of knowing your business. I hope this final chapter has not scared you off. Yes, levers can be problematic if they're not strong enough. However, they can also be wonderfully advantageous to your business. All you have to do is to maintain up-to-date, accurate insights into your business. Understanding the human, operational, and financial levers you have at your disposal is the first step to ensuring your shovel is strong enough to heave out any rock that you might strike in the dirt.

After all you've done to get your business off the ground, from anticipating vectors to building mass, ignoring levers would be a shame. Look back at all you've accomplished (congratulations—it's a feat)! Don't do yourself the disservice now of ignoring those valuable levers. Think back to that great success you aspired to when you had that first tiny kernel of a business idea. Leveraging your business may help you achieve that vision. After all you've accomplished, your levers will help you keep your business moving in a powerful way. Make the most of them.

🧪 IN YOUR LAB

At the beginning of this chapter, I asked you to consider what sources of leverage you have in your business. In addition to identifying those levers, you also must determine how strong they are. These resources can help as you figure it out:

- **Energy Health Check:** Check in with yourself—again. How is your entrepreneurial energy doing since you began your journey? Give it regular care (which could mean taking a break)!

- **Workplace Environment Survey:** Is your team still happy as your business changes and grows? Are they strong and resilient enough to manage changes as they come? Check in with them just as often as you check in with yourself.

- **Client Satisfaction Survey:** Keep getting feedback from customers, again and again and again and … well, you get the picture! Is your bond with your customers strong enough to sustain competitiveness as the market changes, new competitors enter, and so forth?

- **SWOT Analysis:** You likely did a SWOT analysis when you were just getting your business off the ground—and as you were gaining momentum. Again, this is a process you should revisit often. How can you leverage your business SWOT (strengths, weaknesses, opportunities, and threats)?

- **Financial Health Check:** How is your business doing financially? This tool can give you a better sense of overall financial performance, beyond profit margins alone, so you can see where changes need to be made.

- **Financial Performance One-Pager:** A simplified presentation of your business's financial performance can serve all kinds of purposes, from sharing with potential investors to simply giving yourself an easy overview.

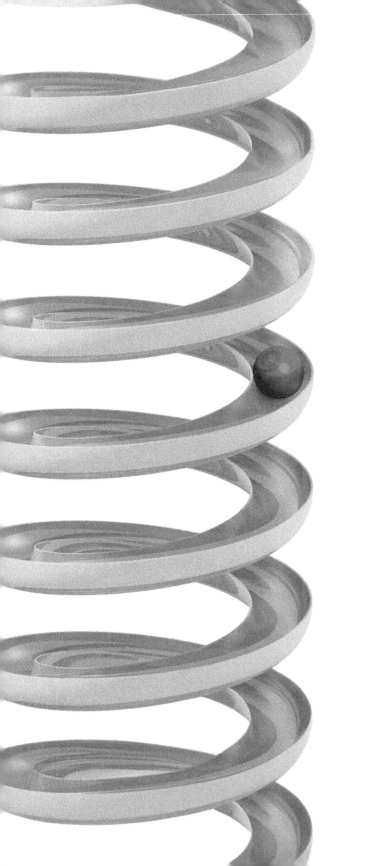

CONCLUSION

I have fond memories of riding my bike as a kid and feeling the wind in my hair, seeing the trees whizzing by me, and hearing a whistling in my ears. That kind of movement was absolutely thrilling to me. Some people are truly gifted at stillness, even thriving in it. But, generally speaking, I think most human beings innately take to the state of being in motion.

It's no surprise. After all, the natural world that we humans inhabit is always in movement. In my mind, physics, the natural science of matter, is all about that motion. From buzzing molecules with their vibrational energy to different types of matter bonding together, the world—even that infinitesimal world we can't see with the naked eye—is just always on the go. How very exciting that is.

Physics governs the natural world and us humans, as part of that natural world. We can't dispute the laws of momentum or force or velocity. So, if physics governs all that we do in the world—why not in the business world too? I'm convinced that the principles of physics can be applied to business—perhaps with this book, I've convinced you too.

It's unlikely that every chapter of this book is relevant for you—but maybe one or two chapters stand out and can help you. Whether you're worried about building density in your organization through appropriate hiring or trying to figure out how to financially leverage your business, I hope some of the principles of Bizzics prove useful to you.

That said, Bizzics is only one road map to business success. If you come away with nothing else from this book, I hope it is a greater awareness of the many resources you have at your disposal as a small business owner. I have mentioned some books that may prove useful to you, including these: *The E-Myth Revisited*, by Michael E. Gerber; *Leadership Is an Art*, by Max De Pree; *On Fire at Work: How Great Companies Ignite Passion in Their People without Burning Them Out*, by Eric Chester; *Everyone Communicates, Few Connect*, by John C. Maxwell; and *Profit First*, by Mike Michalowicz.

You will also find tools and templates on the Bizzics website. I further invite you to join our Bizzics community on Mighty Networks, where you can engage other business owners in discussion about the topics covered in this book—plus other issues related to small business ownership.

There are also many other wonderful organizations you can seek guidance from, including the US SBA, the US Chamber of Commerce—and, of course, your community bank. Having spent the majority of my career in banking, advising small business owners, I know some banks have wonderful resources for this audience.

Starting a business is a courageous step. Don't hesitate to seek support on the journey. Don't be shy to share that entrepreneurial energy. That's how you'll get others buzzing with excitement about your business, which can help you keep moving toward that holy grail, momentum. And in business, just as in the natural world, it's all about momentum.

I know that my most sincere and heartfelt wish for you is the joy of the journey, the fulfillment of your own unique desire to help people in a way that is authentic and unforgettable. Long after the product is consumed or service rendered, the energy of your presence remains with the people you served.

Stay well—and keep moving! I am pulling for you!

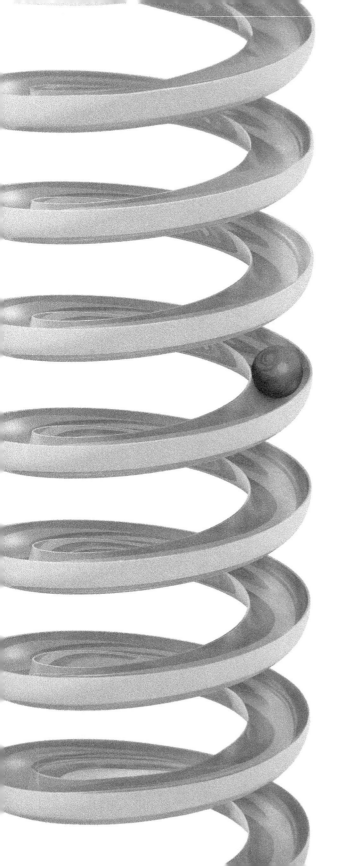

ABOUT THE AUTHOR

Chip Higgins grew up in Winston-Salem, North Carolina, the unassuming home of the Krispy Kreme doughnut—and textiles, tobacco, and banking giants. After earning a bachelor's degree in economics and an MBA, both from University of North Carolina at Chapel Hill, Chip forged a thirty-five-year career in banking. Chip's passion has always been serving small business owners, first as a lender, then in executive leadership roles with three regional banking firms.

Each regional bank Chip has served has been recognized nationally as high performing by Greenwich Associates, the most highly respected commercial banking research firm in the nation. In 2017, Chip's employer tied for the most Small Business Excellence awards among thousands of banks in the survey universe.

In 2011, Chip's love of leadership development led him to become a founding member of the John Maxwell Team of certified coaches, speakers, and trainers. Chip has trained leaders from the Nashville business community to Uganda, earning Volunteer of the Year from the Nashville Business Incubation Center in 2014 for pro bono leadership development work with small business owners.

Chip is eager to help you build your masterpiece. You may discover that the laws of nature are the most powerful business guides of all.

Printed in the USA
CPSIA information can be obtained
at www.ICGtesting.com
JSHW020933300324
60143JS00004B/12/J